Things
Change

D0063349

Also by David Mamet

Published by Grove Press

AMERICAN BUFFALO

THE CHERRY ORCHARD
by Anton Chekhov (an adaptation)

GLENGARRY GLEN ROSS

GOLDBERG STREET: Short Plays and Monologues

HOUSE OF GAMES

A LIFE IN THE THEATRE

REUNION and DARK PONY

SEXUAL PERVERSITY IN CHICAGO and
THE DUCK VARIATIONS

THE SHAWL and PRAIRIE DU CHIEN

SPEED-THE-PLOW

WARM AND COLD (with Donald Sultan)

THE WATER ENGINE and MR. HAPPINESS

THE WOODS, LAKEBOAT, EDMOND

Things Change

A Screenplay Written by

DAVID MAMET

&

SHEL SILVERSTEIN

Grove Press
New York

Published by Grove Press
a division of Wheatland Corporation
841 Broadway
New York, N.Y. 10003

Library of Congress Cataloging-in-Publication Data

Mamet, David.
Things change: a screenplay/by David Mamet and Shel Silverstein. —1st ed.
        p.   cm.
ISBN 0-8021-3047-X
I. Silverstein, Shel. II. Title.
PN 1997.T42854   1988
812'.54—dc19   88-11185
                                CIP

Designed by Irving Perkins Associates

This book is printed on acid-free paper.

Manufactured in the United States of America

First Edition 1988

10 9 8 7 6 5 4 3 2 1

THE CAST

GINO	Don Ameche
JERRY	Joe Mantegna
JOSEPH VINCENT	Robert Prosky
FRANKIE	J. J. Johnston
SILVER	Ricky Jay
MR. GREEN	Mike Nussbaum
SHOE REPAIR STORE OWNER	Jack Wallace
BUTLER	Dan Conway
MISS BATES	Willo Varsi Hausman
GAILE, THE HOUSEMAID	Gail Silver
RAMONE	Len Hodera
BELLENZA	Josh Conescu
MARCOTTI	Adam Bitterman
NO PALS	Merrill Holtzman
NED, THE CHICAGO BODYGUARD	Kenny Lilliebridge
SCARFACE	Chuck Stransky
BILLY DRAKE	W. H. Macy
HOTEL MANAGER	J. T. Walsh
ASSISTANT MANAGER	Jordan Lage
RANDY	Steve Goldstein
CHAMBERMAID	Sarah Potok
BELLBOY 1	Robert Bella
BELLBOY 2	Robert Ostrovsky
MANICURIST	Melissa Bruder
HABERDASHER	Patrick O'Neill
JACKIE SHORE	Jonathan Katz
PIT BOSS	Lionel Smith
CASHIER	Scott Zigler
WHEEL OF FORTUNE LADY	Felicity Huffman
COCKTAIL WAITRESS	Mary Bernadette McCann
PATTY	Patricia Wolff
ROY	G. Roy Levin
ANDY	Andy Potok
THÉO	Théo Cohan
ALLEN	Allen Soule
BURT	Burton Zahler
TEXAS HIGH ROLLER	Derek Hill

PATTY, ROY, ANDY, THÉO, ALLEN, BURT } *Casino Gamblers*

MAÎTRE D' 1	James Donovan
MAÎTRE D' 2	Ken Koc
STAGE MANAGER	Clark Gregg
CHERRY	Sarah Eckhardt
GRACE	Karen Kohlhaas
KENNY	Vincent Guastaferro
HARRY HARDWARE	Christopher Kaldor
ANNA	Natalia Nogulich
COOK	Val Clemmer
ITALIAN DON	John Cardinale
WILLIE, THE TEXAS DON	Bill Bagwell
HOWARD, THE NEW YORK DON	Howard Rosenstone
GAS STATION ATTENDANT	Paul Butler
BAILIFF	Jerry Graff
JUDGE	Dick Cusack

THE CREDITS

Produced by	Michael Hausman
Directed by	David Mamet
Written by	David Mamet
	and Shel Silverstein
Director of Photography	Juan Ruiz Anchia
Music by	Alaric Jans
Edited by	Trudy Ship
Production Designer	Michael Merritt
Costume Designer	Nan Cibula
Unit Production Manager	Michael Hausman
First Assistant Director	
and Associate Producer	Ned Dowd
Second Assistant Director	Cara Giallanza
Second Second Assistant Director	Lynn Wegenka
Script Supervisor	Anne Rapp
Location Manager	Ron Rotholz
Post Production Supervisor	Rachel Cline
Production Accountant	Kevin Hyman
Assistant to Mr. Mamet	Patricia Wolff
Production Office Coordinator	Mary Lou Devlin
Assistant Production Office	
Coordinator	Cathy Sarkowsky
Chicago Location Manager	Randy Ostrow
Assistant Accountant	Christie Christl
Casting	Cyrena Hausman
Casting Assistant	Ruth Barnes
First Assistant Camera	Bob Hall
Second Assistant Camera	Henry Cline
Still Photographer	Stephen Vaughan

Chicago Still Photographer	Deana Newcomb
Gaffer	Ian Kincaid
Best Boy	David Dubois
Key Dolly Grip	Chris A. Centrella
Best Boy	Hugh McCallum
Sound Mixer	John Pritchett
Boom Operator	Joel Shryack
Cable	Laura Derrick
	Dale Janus
Assistant Production Designer	Shawn Hausman
Set Decorator	Derek R. Hill
Lead Man	Grey Smith
Set Dresser	Kim Hobbs
Property Master	Samara Schaffer
Wardrobe Supervisor	Mark Burchard
Wardrobe	Bill Edwards
Makeup	Pamela Westmore
Hair Stylist	Erin Lyons
Public Relations	Nancy Seltzer
	and Associates, Inc.

Things
Change

Interior: Music Store—Day

Fade In: A man's back. As he turns, camera reveals he is playing a mandolin.

He walks across the room playing. He stops and takes another mandolin off the rack, replacing it with the one he was playing. He continues playing on the second mandolin.

He goes to the counter, behind which a woman stands.

The camera tracks past him onto two men standing in front of a window looking out. These men are Frankie and Silver.

They look out to the street.

Their point of view. Gino comes out of a door across the street. He starts walking down the sidewalk.

Silver looks at Frankie. Frankie nods to him.

They exit.

Gino continues down the sidewalk.

They cross the street and follow him.

Gino continues. They continue to follow.

Gino continues. They continue to follow him around a corner.

Exterior: Shoe Repair Store—Day

Gino walks across the street and enters the shoe repair store. Frankie and Silver follow behind him.

Interior: Shoe Repair Store

Frankie and Silver enter the store. The owner looks up.

OWNER: May I help you?

Silver shakes his head "no." He sees Gino come out from the back room and go over to the shoeshine stand. Silver goes over to him.

SILVER: A friend of ours would like to speak to you this evening.

Silver takes out a wallet and takes a card from it. He hands it to Gino with a hundred-dollar bill. Gino takes it and looks at Silver.

GINO: I just shine shoes.

SILVER: There'll be shoes there.

Silver walks back to the door and he and Frankie walk out of the store. Gino looks after them.

Interior: Living Room—A Mansion—Night

Camera on Gino's shoebox, next to Gino's legs. He is seated in a chair in the living room. We tilt up to his face as he is watching a bodyguard, Scarface, at the closed doors to the room. He hears the sound of doors opening and looks over to see.

Silver and Mr. Green open the doors from the study. They step forward. Green goes and sits down on the couch. Silver steps forward and stands behind Green at the back of the couch.

Angle. Gino, unmoving.

Angle. Silver and Mr. Green at the couch.

SILVER: Two weeks ago a man named Aaronberg was shot to death, the corner of Racine and Belden—this is public knowledge. Two people saw the crime, and this was also in the papers. This is public knowledge. What I'm going to tell you now is not public knowledge. Do you understand?

Pause. Gino looks down. He nods his head.

Good. The act was committed by a person unknown. "A Man in a Gray Overcoat." Unfortunately, a friend of ours has been mistakenly identified as the man who did the murder.

MR. GREEN: Show him the picture.

Silver goes over to a large, framed photograph on a table. He picks it up and turns to Gino.

SILVER: This is the man who has been mistakenly accused.

Silver hands Gino the photograph. Gino holds it up. We see the picture.

Insert. The photograph.

Gino and the man in the photograph are very similar looking. Gino has a droopy moustache where the man in the photo has a pencil moustache, their hair styles are different, otherwise they look the same.

Angle. Gino holding the photo. Silver sits in the chair next to Gino.

MR. GREEN: Do you understand?

Gino looks at him, nods.

SILVER: To prevent a grave injustice from being done. To protect an innocent man (*gestures at photo*), someone must confess to the crime . . . someone who looks like . . . (*Gestures at photo.*) This man would plead guilty to murder, and would, unfortunately, spend a term of three to five years in prison. (*Beat.*) To such a person we are prepared to pay . . . (*Scribbles on a pad.*) This amount of money per year. For each year he spent in prison.

   Angle. Gino. He looks at the paper.

MR. GREEN (*shrugs*): You could say you were in a prison now. (*He nods sympathetically.*) In three years . . . You must have a dream . . . do you have a dream?

Gino nods.

And what is that dream?

GINO: A boat.

MR. GREEN: A boat . . .

   Angle. Gino sitting across from Mr. Green.

GINO: A fishing boat.

MR. GREEN: Your dream is a fishing boat.

GINO: In Sicily . . .

MR. GREEN: In three years, you could have that fishing boat. You could earn yourself that boat. If you stay in your shoe store, what will you have in three years?

Angle. Gino, unable to decide.

SILVER: What do you have in three years? What do you have now . . .?

Angle. Mr. Green looking at Gino.

Gino still cannot decide.

MR. GREEN: Will you help me?

Gino hesitates—shakes his head "no."

Mr. Green shrugs, leans back.

MR. GREEN: No? It's alright. Shine 'em uppa, Joe . . .

SILVER (*sotto, to Gino*): You've just made a grave mistake.

Mr. Green summons Silver. Starts giving orders.

SILVER: Shine the shoes.

MR. GREEN: Alright. Call Marty in Detroit, I want to see him as soon as possible . . . And get me whatsisname downtown . . .

Silver, who has brought the shoebox and placed it at the feet of Mr. Green, goes into the study and starts making phone calls.

Mr. Green gestures to Gino, who has gotten out of his chair. He is confused as to what to do.

Watch out for the socks—those are cashmere socks. (*To Silver:*) Get whatsisname downtown.

Miss Bates enters the room from the hallway. Gino watches her. She goes and whispers something to Mr. Green, then crosses to a table with a jar of cigarettes. She takes one and then looks around for a light.

Gino comes forward to shine the shoes, but sees the chance to light Miss Bates's cigarette. He picks up a lighter from the coffee table and holds it up to her.

She starts to get a light, but notices his dirty hands and draws back. She gives him a drop-dead look and turns and goes into the office where she finds a match on the desk.

During this Mr. Green has continued giving orders.

MR. GREEN: Tell 'em I need a guy, I need a friend . . . He'll know what it's about, tell him I need this in a hurry. And call Plesetska in the twenty-eighth district.

Mr. Green turns back to Gino.

Let's go, let's go, boy. We wanna get you back to your shoeshine stand . . .

Gino kneels down and opens his box. Mr. Green stands up, giving Gino a contemptuous look and walks into the office. Gino slowly stands and starts to leave.

Gino stops and looks into the study as Miss Bates walks from the study and passes him, giving him a withering look.

Gino is hurt. He turns to Mr. Green and Silver.

GINO: I do it.

Mr. Green and Silver turn and stare at him. Silver puts down the phone. Mr. Green comes to Gino.

MR. GREEN: Thank you. (*He takes an old silver coin off his watch fob and holds it up to Gino.*) This is a Sicilian coin. The Sicilian people say "A big man . . ."

Silver, realizing that Mr. Green may be about to say the wrong thing to Gino, interrupts Mr. Green.

SILVER: Excuse me.

Mr. Green continues.

MR. GREEN: "A big man knows the value of a small coin." My friendship is a small coin, but it is all I have to offer you. Thank you.

He places the coin in Gino's hand and closes his hand. Mr. Green leads Gino to the desk and motions to Silver.

The paper.

Silver takes the typed confession out of a manila envelope and puts it on the desk in front of Gino. He hands Gino a pen.

SILVER: Sign here.

Gino signs the document.

MR. GREEN: And now . . .

Silver takes a silk scarf out of the folder. He lays it on the desk and unwraps it, revealing a pistol. Gino looks at Mr. Green, confused.

We need your fingerprints.

Silver opens the cartridge on the gun.

SILVER: Pick up the gun and close it.

Gino takes the gun out of the silk scarf, grips it, replaces it. The Don nods. He motions to the butler who has come in with a tray of drinks. Mr. Green and Gino each take a glass.

MR. GREEN: To my new friend.

They toast and drink.

Interior: Hallway/Kitchen—Mr. Green's House—Night

The butler exits the living room. He walks through the large hallway into the narrow corridor to the kitchen. A maid passes by him as he goes into the kitchen and lights a cigarette.

In the kitchen, eight beefy bodyguards sitting around. Frankie comes into the room holding pay envelopes.

FRANKIE: Bellenza . . .

BELLENZA: Yeah.

Frankie tosses him an envelope.

FRANKIE: Good work you done on that last thing.

BELLENZA: Thank you, Frank.

FRANKIE: Marcotti . . .

MARCOTTI: Yo.

FRANKIE (*of envelope*): Heavy—whattaya, getting ambition? (*He throws the envelope to Marcotti.*)

MARCOTTI: Just tryin' to do the job, Frank.

Frankie passes out some other envelopes and thanks each man. He stops when he sees the name on the next envelope.

FRANKIE: We got a . . . what is this . . . Jerry something or other working here?

Jerry, a man in his late thirties, at the back of the room, washing dishes in a deep sink.

I thought we sent him down to the Farm team . . .

RAMONE: Why was that Frank?

FRANKIE: It seems he can't follow orders . . . !

Laughter from the group. They look at Jerry.

RAMONE: Can't follow orders? What, is the guy a team player or what?

FRANKIE: No, it would seem not.

Frankie has walked in to where Jerry is washing dishes and he drops his pay envelope on the counter.

BELLENZA: That's a shame, Frank.

FRANKIE: Yes, I agree with you.

NO PALS: No pay, no pals, no prospects.

RAMONE: What kind a guy is that?

Jerry, hearing all this, picks up the pay envelope. It is empty. He tears it in half. The maid, Gaile, carries a dirty skillet into the sink area and hands it to Jerry.

GAILE: You think you can get this clean?

Jerry looks dejected.

Interior: Kitchen

The men in the kitchen. A few minutes later. In the middle of a conversation . . .

RAMONE: Thirty-fifth and Halsted.

FRANKIE: The guy on the corner?

RAMONE: Yeah.

NO PALS: I know that guy.

MARCOTTI: Oh yeah.

FRANKIE: Forget him. There's nothing . . .

Silver comes into the room and calls to Frankie.

SILVER: Frankie.

Frankie goes to Silver and they hold a whispered conversation. Silver gives Frankie an envelope containing the photograph we saw in the living room. Silver leaves. Frankie turns to Jerry.

FRANKIE: Hey Cinderella . . . comeere . . .

Jerry looks up, steps forward, and takes off his apron.

Interior: The Hallway—Night

The guards open the door and Gino and Mr. Green come out into the hallway. Scarface brings Gino his coat and helps him on with it.

Silver comes from the kitchen corridor and gets the gray overcoat and hat out of the closet. He brings them and shows them to Gino. They go out of the hallway into the kitchen corridor.

They come into the kitchen as Frankie is pulling on his coat and Jerry is in the kitchen. Gino almost bumps into Jerry. Mr. Green leads Gino out the door.

Silver calls Jerry and Frankie together and gives them more instructions.

Exterior: Mansion—Night

The steps to the mansion, the car outside, the bodyguards standing in the doorway of the house. The Don comes out with Gino, they shake hands. Gino starts down the steps to the car. He turns and gives a nod to Mr. Green, then goes to the car. Mr. Green goes back into the house as Frankie comes out followed by Jerry.

FRANKIE: Now you do this one right.

JERRY: I'm doing it right. I'm getting off probation.

FRANKIE: Just do this, and then we'll see . . .

Jerry goes down the steps and motions Gino into the waiting car. They drive away. The bodyguards close the gate and go back into the house.

Interior: Cheap Hotel Room—Night

Empty coffee cups. The shoeshine box by the side of the bed. The gray overcoat on a hanger, hung on a door. Jerry lounges on a bed, holding a list. Gino sitting by the bureau. Jerry reads from the list.

JERRY: Why did you kill him?

GINO (*reciting*): He was a No-Good Son of a Bitch.

JERRY: . . . and (*Pause.*)

GINO: . . . he . . .

JERRY: . . . you owed him money.

GINO: I owed him money.

JERRY: How much did you owe him?

GINO: Fifteen hundred dollar.

JERRY: That's right. What did you do with the money?

GINO: I lost it at the racetrack.

JERRY: What time was it you killed him? Hold on, you know that one. How many times did you shoot him?

GINO: Three times.

JERRY: Yeah, don't get it too pat, three or four . . .

GINO: Three or four times I shot him. That son of a bitch.

They sit there. Jerry nods. Puts down the list. Beat. Gets up.

You no want to do some more?

JERRY: Na. You know it. (*Beat.*) You know it.

Jerry walks over to the television set, turns it on. Turns it off.

Hey, this is *ridiculous*. You're going to jail for ten years. What, what do you want to do?

*Jerry picks up one of the hotel "Things to See in Chicago" magazines
. . . starts leafing through it.*

What do you, you want to get a couple of *broads* . . . ? You what,
you want to see a show?

GINO: Na . . .

JERRY: Hey . . . I'll get you *tickets* to something . . . we'll . . .

GINO: I . . . They, they say I am supposed to do?

JERRY: They? There *is* no "they." *I* am they. What do you want
to do?

Beat.

GINO: Could we maybe . . . could we, could we take a walk by the
beach? Would that be okay?

JERRY: "Okay?" "Okay?" I'll show you what's "Okay." *I'll* show you
what's "Okay."

He looks down at the magazine in his hand.

> *Angle. Jerry's hand holding the magazine. On the left-hand
> page, listings of "What to Do in Chicago," on the right-hand
> page, a full-page spread. A show girl, "While in Lake Tahoe,
> Visit Our Sister Hotel, the Fabulous* Galaxy.*"*

Exterior: Lake Tahoe Airport—Day

*Jet door opens. Jerry and Gino come out, walk down the ramp to a
beautiful, crisp, clear Tahoe morning. They breathe in the air.*

As they walk toward the terminal, a sleek, private jet taxis into position to receive passengers, its door opens, the ramp descends, and two bodyguard types appear at the top of the ramp, obviously waiting for someone.

Interior: Airport

Jerry and Gino are walking through the airport.

JERRY: You like to travel?

GINO: Sure.

JERRY: Okay, good.

GINO: I like.

JERRY: Good.

They walk outside onto the curb.

JERRY: Two days, you understand, a little fun, a little memory, then back to Chicago.

GINO: Back to Chicago, I shoot the sonofabitch in the heart . . .

JERRY: And when I say it, out here, *do* it.

GINO: . . . You the boss.

JERRY: I *am* the boss. You keep that clear, we're going to get on fine.

A big white stretch limo is sitting at the curb. The driver, Billy Drake, jumps out of the driver's seat and races around to hold open the back door.

Two bodyguard types get out, followed by a small dark man in a business suit. The bodyguards rush the man into the airport; Billy Drake salutes. Drake spies Gino and Jerry and comes over to them.

BILLY DRAKE: Jerry! Howya doin' ? What are YOU doin' here . . . ?

JERRY: Hey, how are *you*, I'm doin' fine. How should I be doin' ?

BILLY DRAKE: You know. I heard you mucked up back there last month.

JERRY: What does that mean?

BILLY DRAKE: I heard they slapped your wrist.

JERRY: What wrist?

BILLY DRAKE: I heard you had to Stay After School. You couldn't obey *orders*.

JERRY (*getting a bit mad*): "Stay After School" ? "Stay After School"? Are you *joking* me . . . Does this look like staying after school?

He points to Gino. Billy Drake looks at Gino. Beat. Billy Drake moves in to Jerry. Gino moves to them.

BILLY DRAKE (*softly, respectfully*): Who *is* it . . . ?

JERRY: If you *don't* know, then you *shouldn't* know.

Billy Drake gets a little bit flustered. Beat.

BILLY DRAKE: Uh, you staying at The Hotel?

JERRY: Uh, yeah. We're staying at The Hotel.

BILLY DRAKE: You got a *ride* . . . ?

JERRY: . . . I think they're sending somebody down to . . .

BILLY DRAKE: . . . *hey, get in* . . . (*He indicates the car.*)

He opens the door to the limo. Jerry hangs back.

Naaa, get in . . .

Billy Drake takes Gino to the back door, takes the coats, holds open the back door. Beat. Jerry nods, gestures Gino to get in. Gino gets in the limo. Then Billy gets in. Jerry reacts, gets in. Car drives away.

Interior: Limo—Back Seat—Day

Gino sitting alone in the back of the limo, a bag of grapes next to him. He sees a cigarette box, takes it down, opens it, takes out a cigarette. He starts to light it, then puts it in his pocket. He thinks a moment, then puts the cigarette back in the box and replaces the box.

He takes out a grape from the bag and eats it.

He looks out the windows.

The partition between the back and the driver's seat comes down to reveal the driver and Jerry sitting next to him.

BILLY DRAKE: Hey, you know, the rap was you got in some deep powder back there. I heard they put you on probation.

JERRY: Well, you can't believe everything you hear. Sometimes they put out a *story, you* know . . .

BILLY DRAKE: Uh huh. And so, what, and so you're . . .

JERRY: What I am is what you see.

BILLY DRAKE (*beat*): And so, your guy, he's big back there . . . ?

JERRY: Babe, this is the guy, *behind* the guy, *behind* the guy . . .
But what I got to *tell* you, is, I cannot *talk* about it.

BILLY DRAKE: I understand.

JERRY: He wants to come out here, a quiet weekend . . .

BILLY DRAKE: I understand . . .

JERRY: . . . a bit of this, a bit of that . . . no fuss . . .

BILLY DRAKE: I understand.

*He puts on his dark glasses to indicate that the case is closed and
that he will go on with the program.*

> *Angle—Point of view. The white limo approaching, gliding
> up to the curb.*

Exterior: Galaxy Hotel—Day

*The car park attendants snap to attention as the limo stops. Billy
Drake quickly gets out of the front seat. He comes around, pushes
bellhop out of the way.*

> *Angle. Jerry gets out, Billy Drake comes around to the back
> door to open it. Gino gets out.*

JERRY: Billy, thanks. Pal.

BILLY DRAKE: Walk you in . . .

Billy takes Gino's arm and starts to walk him toward the hotel; Jerry holds back.

JERRY: Thanks, pal, I'll take it from Here On In . . .

BILLY DRAKE: No problem. Right this way.

Camera follows them into the hotel.

Interior: Galaxy Hotel—Day

JERRY: I'm tryin' a keep a Low Profile, you understand, we like to Go In Quiet . . .

BILLY DRAKE (*simultaneously with "Quiet"*): Can we get some attention here please!

They arrive at the check-in counter. A clerk looks up.

CLERK: May I help you . . . ?

Billy Drake clears his throat, points behind the clerk to the manager, who is talking on the phone. The manager looks over.

MANAGER (*into phone*): Excuse me, I'll call you back.

   Angle. The group at the check-in counter. The manager pushes the clerk aside. All smiles.

Good morning, sir. How good to have you with us. (*He brushes the check-in form aside.*) Shall we go right up to the room?

The manager reaches behind him to the key rack. Puts his hand on a key.

Angle—Close-up. The manager looks questioningly at Billy Drake.

Angle—Point of view. Billy Drake shakes his head—"No, not good enough."

Angle. The manager reaches for a key on a higher rack. Billy Drake nods that this is acceptable.

We're going upstairs!

The assistants scurry off as the manager comes from behind the counter.

Welcome to the Galaxy. (*Calling after his assistants:*) Please call upstairs and tell them that our friends are coming.

He points Gino and Jerry toward the elevator. Billy Drake is left behind.

BILLY DRAKE (*to the retreating Gino*): Anything you need, in Lake Tahoe, sir, I'd be honored if you'd ask for me, Billy Drake . . .

The entourage is walking toward the elevators. The manager hangs back, gestures to Drake—"Who is he . . . ?"

From Chicago. Very big.

Drake gestures—"Trust me . . ." The manager nods—"Say no more."

Interior: Hotel Elevator Bank—Corridor

Randy, the concierge, is on the phone.

RANDY: Yes sir, I understand. Absolutely. I understand completely. (*He hears the elevator bell.*) Ah, here they are now. (*He hangs up, looks at the elevators.*)

Jerry and Gino come out of the elevators, followed by two bellboys from downstairs. They come to the gates.

JERRY: Hi.

RANDY (*opens gates*): Welcome to the Criterion Floor, Mr. . . .

JERRY: Johnson. Look. It's a good idea . . . It's very important that nobody knows that Mr. Johnson is here.

RANDY: I understand.

They continue down the hall to the suite.

RANDY: I'm your butler, my name is Randy, and I'll be at your disposal Twenty-Four Hours A Day . . .

Interior: Hotel Suite

Randy opens the door, Jerry and Gino enter a magnificently appointed, huge duplex hotel suite. The bellboys cross into the room. Randy shuts door and enters the room.

JERRY: *Stai calmo, lo paccio io.* [I'm gonna handle this.]

GINO: *Come vuole lei.* [Anything you say.]

They cross into room.

RANDY: Any help you need, in travel arrangements, special dietary preparation, cleaning, mending, shoeshine, shopping, or any other aid that you require, don't hesitate to ring. The manager informs me that all of our staff have been advised that any wish expressed by you or Mr. Johnson . . .

JERRY: No, no, no, no, nobody *is to know* that Mr. Johnson . . .

RANDY: Believe me, believe me, we understand. Your privacy will be respected . . .

JERRY: We're here for Two Days Quiet, a little low-profile relaxation . . .

RANDY: I completely understand. We of the Galaxy appreciate and understand your position, believe me.

GINO: I be right back.

He goes through the bedroom to the bathroom. He looks down at the toilet, which is covered by a seat guard.

Back to the living room, where Randy is still talking.

RANDY: . . . additional security in whatever depth or force, telecommunications, telefax, secretarial, or legal services. I am a notary should you require it . . .

RANDY (*to bellboy*): Where are the bags . . . ? Where are the bags . . . ?

JERRY: We, uh, lost the bags on a connection. Look:

RANDY: Our stores and shops are yours, whatever you require, go down, or ring, and they'll have it sent up.

JERRY: That's very kind of you, but . . .

RANDY: Credit in the casino, whatever you require . . . in financial services we have twenty-four-hour access to a tickertape of the major markets.

Back to Gino.

The toilet is flushing. Gino replaces the seat guard.

Back to living room.

Gino enters the living room.

RANDY: . . . tickets for the show, Jackie Shore tonight in the Constellation Room or tickets for any other show in town. (*Hands Jerry book.*) The sights and sounds of Lake Tahoe . . . and here is my card. I'm at that number, or they'll beep me, any time, *any* time at all . . . Mr. Johnson, any questions about the room? (*Gino gestures "no."*) I believe we've anticipated your tobacco requirements. Anything we've missed, let me know . . .

Camera follows Gino on his voyage of discovery. He disappears into the sauna room. He turns on the light and looks at the Roman hot tub, turns off the light and leaves. He comes out and goes back into living room.

RANDY: . . . it is a pleasure and an honor having you as a guest of the Galaxy and of the Criterion Floor. My name is Randy, and whatever I can do to make your stay more enjoyable, it will be my honor and pleasure to serve you. The concierge desk and our kitchen are at your disposal, and should you wish to shop, our shops and stores are open to you, on a private basis, twenty-four hours a day.

JERRY: . . . shops and stores, uh huh. But where do you send the bill?

RANDY: Oh, no, sir. There is no bill. Your money is no good in this hotel.

Randy bows himself out. Gino and Jerry look at each other.

Interior: Manicure Shop

A *manicurist finishes giving Gino a manicure.*

MANICURIST: Mr. Johnson, you have beautiful hands.

HABERDASHER: Yes, and a lovely treatment of the hands, if I may say so, sir; clean, without being austere.

Gino turns around in his chair. He looks at his hands. He gets up out of the chair, nods. The haberdasher helps Gino on with the jacket of the new suit he now wears.

HABERDASHER: Mr. Johnson, it has been a pleasure.

Gino buttons his jacket. He looks at Jerry, who is also completely re-attired in new and very expensive clothing. Jerry rises, goes and stands by Gino. He picks off a piece of lint. He turns to the door. The two of them leave in unison.

Suddenly Jerry runs back in, gets the airline tickets out of his old jacket pocket, puts them in his pocket, walks out.

Gino comes back in, gets a hanky, puts it in his jacket pocket. He leaves.

They walk together out of the hall.

Interior: Galaxy Hallway—Day

Open on poster of Jackie Shore.

JERRY (*off screen*): Okay, we're here on a *pass*, huh . . . ?

Pull back to reveal the hallway; Jerry and Gino walk into the frame.

JERRY: But clothes don't make the man. *I* Make the Man. Y'unner-
stand me, just because we got new clothes . . .

*Jerry pats himself down, finds the airline tickets, relaxes, replaces
the tickets.*

A cocktail waitress comes into the frame.

COCKTAIL WAITRESS: Something to drink, gentlemen?

GINO: A scotch.

COCKTAIL WAITRESS (*to Jerry*): Sir . . . ?

JERRY: Nothing for me. I'm here to gamble . . .

Jerry and Gino walk out of the frame.

Interior: Casino

   Angle—Point of view. Gino and Jerry walk into the casino.

They pass a wheel of fortune. Allen is playing.

ALLEN: Put five on nine, five on nineteen, and five for you, dealer,
spin it!

*Wheel of fortune lady spins. They walk to a slot machine, and Gino
tries to pull the lever.*

JERRY: You have to put money in it.

They walk over to the cashier window.

JERRY: Hey!

CASHIER: I'll be with you in a moment.

JERRY: Gimme twenty dollars.

Jerry turns his attention to Gino.

JERRY: So we're gonna have two wonderful days . . .

GINO: I understand.

JERRY: We aren't going to "go crazy" . . .

GINO: Two days, then we go back to Chicago . . .

JERRY: Well, that's absolutely right.

A pretty girl walks by. Jerry and Gino, smitten, turn to look at her.

GINO: Ten o'clock Monday morning, twenty-eighth district . . . I wear the gray overcoat . . . I see the sonabitch, three shots *right here*. (*He pats his heart.*)

JERRY: So how do you feel, tight but aggressive?

GINO: Okay.

JERRY: Good.

CASHIER: May I help you?

JERRY: Yeah, give me twenty dollars.

The assistant manager walks up.

ASSISTANT MANAGER: Everything alright, gentlemen?

JERRY: No, we just . . .

ASSISTANT MANAGER (*to cashier*): Whatever credit these gentlemen require—There's no limit, and I mean *no* limit.

The cashier pushes the chips across to them.

CASHIER: Twenty dollars.

JERRY: Yeah, no, no, I think . . . I'm making a joke, here, just gimme a thousand . . . gimme a thousand bucks . . . uh . . . *tab* it.

The cashier nods, starts counting.

ASSISTANT MANAGER: Would you like a table for the late show, Jackie Shore, Constellation Room . . . ?

JERRY (*remonstrating with a gesture*): In the *back* . . .

The assistant manager nods—"Of course." A large tray of chips is pushed to Jerry by the cashier.

CASHIER: . . . one thousand dollars.

JERRY (*offhand*): Thanks.

A cocktail waitress calls the assistant manager aside.

If you got the Name, go get the Game . . . let's gamble.

GINO: Okay.

Gino reaches for the chip tray with the thousand dollars in it. Jerry moves it away.

JERRY: No, hey, that's for "show"— Play what you got in your pockets . . .

Gino nods.

ASSISTANT MANAGER (*following them*): . . . and if there's anything at *all* that I can do for you . . .

Jerry nods him away.

Gino puts money in a slot machine. The slot stops. No winner. Gino shrugs.

GINO: I never win nothing.

JERRY: Well, maybe we can fix that.

GINO: Oh, no, Jerry, not even *you* can fix something like that.

JERRY: "Not even me," eh . . . ?

GINO: Not even you.

JERRY: Not even someone like me . . . (*He hands Gino some change.*) Here. Put it in. Put it in.

Jerry goes over to the assistant manager. Camera follows, leaving Gino playing the slot machines in the background.

(*To assistant manager:*) Hey, wait a second, there is something you can do for me . . .

   Angle. Gino.

Gino puts three quarters in, pulls, nothing. He reaches in his pocket and pulls out three more quarters and the Sicilian coin. He takes a moment to look at it, sighs, puts the Sicilian coin away, puts in the first quarter and pulls.

Angle. Jerry and the assistant manager.

JERRY: I'd like to give Mr. Johnson a little . . . "treat" . . .

ASSISTANT MANAGER: Absolutely, sir . . .

JERRY: Can we, can we, could we arrange for him, as a "lark," to "win," a little, you know . . .

ASSISTANT MANAGER: . . . to "win" . . .

JERRY: . . . just a little . . .

ASSISTANT MANAGER: . . . to win in the Casino . . .

JERRY: . . . just a little, just fifty, a hundred dollars, as a "thrill," you know, could you do that?

ASSISTANT MANAGER: . . . well . . .

JERRY: . . . and whatever it is, I'll make it up . . .

ASSISTANT MANAGER: . . . you're saying that you'll pay it back . . .

JERRY: . . . that's what I'm saying . . .

ASSISTANT MANAGER: Alright.

Jerry walks back toward Gino. The assistant manager calls "Mr. Davis," the pit boss, over and they mumble to each other.

JERRY: Broke so soon?

GINO: Yep.

JERRY: Hey, the slots are cold. Let's try something else.

GINO: Okay.

As they turn we see the pit boss whisper "twelve" to the assistant manager. Jerry and Gino walk toward them. The assistant manager leads the group to the private roulette room and takes down the rope. The assistant manager whispers "twelve" to Jerry, who nods. The pit boss changes his jacket for a dealer's vest, then follows. They all go inside. The assistant manager puts the rope back and stands.

JERRY (*to pit boss*): This table open . . . ?

PIT BOSS (*as he takes down the rope*): Yes, it is. (*He clears table.*)

JERRY: Okay, you got *black*, you got *red*, you got *numbers* . . . whaddaya wanna bet . . . ?

GINO: I take black.

JERRY: Take a number, take a number . . . Take a number.

GINO: Okay.

JERRY: You pick a number, it hits, it pays thirty-five to one, put five bucks on a number.

Pit boss spins wheel.

GINO: We partners.

JERRY: Naa. It's yours . . .

GINO: We partners, whatever happen, we go Fifty-Fifty. Okay?

JERRY: Yeah, okay.

Gino starts to put his chip on a number.

JERRY: You know what, you know what number I always play? . . .
my *flight* number. What flight did we come in on . . . ?

GINO: I . . .

JERRY: *Twelve,* wasn't it . . . ?

GINO: I, yeah.

JERRY: Yeah, I think that it was flight number twelve.

*Gino takes a five-dollar chip from his pocket and puts it on twelve.
Pit boss rolls ball. They watch the ball.*

*Jackie Shore, the comic, comes up to the assistant manager, draws
him aside.*

JACKIE SHORE: Miles, I gotta talk to you . . .

ASSISTANT MANAGER: Not now, Jackie.

JACKIE SHORE: Babe, I'm not getting the support I need, your new
lighting guy . . .

  Insert. Ball hits number twelve.

PIT BOSS: *Twelve.*

GINO: I win.

JERRY (*to assistant manager*): You see what my friend did . . . !

ASSISTANT MANAGER: Bravo, Mr. Johnson, good play.

JACKIE SHORE (*to assistant manager*): We gotta lose the lighting
guy. He's napping on me up there. I won't say it's *hurting* the show
. . . it's *not* hurting the show . . . but . . .

PIT BOSS: Place your bets . . .

Gino hesitates, takes the tray containing one thousand dollars, and places it on number twelve. The pit boss spins the wheel again.

JACKIE SHORE *(to Jerry)*: You seen the show . . . ? Mr. . . . ? ?

ASSISTANT MANAGER: Mr. Johnson and his people don't want any notice.

JACKIE SHORE: I understand. *(To Jerry:)* Have you seen the show?

Jerry turns to face Jackie Shore and doesn't see Gino.

JERRY: No, I can't say that I have.

JACKIE SHORE: Okay, there's a bit that I do . . . I'm working the crowd.

ASSISTANT MANAGER: This is not the time to, Jackie, this is not the . . .

JACKIE SHORE: I just want to make a point. *(To Jerry:)* A beautiful show, a fine show, well thought out, but if you don't have the support . . . you see that's my theme in what I'm telling you . . . support . . .

PIT BOSS *(voice-over)*: Twelve again . . .

Jerry hears this, turns, and looks at the table. He sees the thousand dollars on twelve.

GINO: I win again!

Jerry walks over to the table.

   Close-up—*The pit boss. His face says* "I think I did the right thing."

Angle—Insert. The ball sitting in number twelve.

Angle—Insert. Number twelve covered by a thousand dollars in chips.

Angle. At the table Gino, chuckling.

How much we win??? How much we win!!!

Pit Boss stacks some black chips.

Angle—Insert. Chips pushed to Gino.

PIT BOSS: Thirty-five thousand dollars.

Angle. The roulette table. Onlookers beginning to crowd around. The pit boss pushing endless stacks of chips toward Gino. The pit boss's face says "I hope I did the right thing."

GINO (*to onlookers*): You fly Number Twelve, you play Number Twelve.

JERRY (*to Gino, sitting him down*): Huh. That's a lot of money . . .

GINO: Oh yeah . . .

JERRY: What do you . . . what number do you want to play *now?*

GINO: Naaa, we got *enough* . . . (*Starts to rake the chips toward himself.*) Come on, I buy you a car . . . ! ! !

JERRY: Uh . . .

Jerry leans into Gino, they go into a conference.

ASSISTANT MANAGER (*voice-over*): Sir . . . ?

JERRY: Yeah, hold on a second . . .

*He leans into his whispered conversation with Gino. Gino looks
perplexed.*

> *Angle. Gino and Jerry get up from the table, Jerry with his arm
> around Gino. They walk to the back part of the room.*

> *Angle. Gino and Jerry.*

Gino . . .

GINO: Yeah. What we do with this money . . . ?

JERRY: Gino, we got to give it back.

Beat.

GINO: Why? I *won* it.

JERRY: Yeah, but, yeah, but . . .

GINO: I *won* the money . . .

JERRY: Yeah, but listen, listen, it's, it's, it's a thing of "hospitality."
We're um, we're "guests" in their hotel, we sure, we could take the
money, it's not a question of the "money" . . . It's just for the sake
of, um, of "honor," to be an honorable guest . . .

Gino hesitates.

GINO: It's not the "money," it's "honor" . . .

JERRY: Um, yeah. Do you, uh, do you understand me?

*Gino turns, walks toward the main casino. Jerry follows. The assis-
tant manager opens the rope. Six people are watching at the rope.*

*Gino continues to walk out into the casino. Jerry and the assistant
manager stop behind him.*

ASSISTANT MANAGER: Excuse me, I have to talk to you.

JERRY: In a minute . . .

ASSISTANT MANAGER: I have to talk to you.

Gino stops and looks off screen left. A cocktail waitress comes up to him.

COCKTAIL WAITRESS: Something to drink, sir?

GINO: Scotch, please.

Gino moves forward.

The cocktail waitress passes by them.

PATTY: What happened?

ANDY: Some guy just won thirty-five grand.

Burt, then Andy and his girl follow Gino. Standing watching are Jerry, assistant manager, pit boss, Texas high roller, Jackie Shore, and others.

   Angle—Point of view. Gino looks at wheel of fortune.

Gino walks up to the wheel of fortune.

GINO: How this game work?

WHEEL OF FORTUNE LADY: Well, we pay one-hundred-to-one. If you bet a dollar and your number wins you win one hundred dollars.

GINO: How much I can bet?

WHEEL OF FORTUNE LADY: Just as advertised, Sir, the wheel of fortune, the Pride of the Galaxy, never refused a bet of any size.

GINO: How much I win if I bet thirty-five thousand dollars?

WHEEL OF FORTUNE LADY: If you bet thirty-five thousand dollars and your number wins, you'd win three million five hundred thousand dollars.

Angle—Insert. Table.

GINO: I bet thirty-five thousand dollars. Put it on number twelve.

The wheel of fortune lady takes a look at the assistant manager. The assistant manager looks to Jerry. Jerry drops his head. The assistant manager looks back to the wheel of fortune lady and shrugs. Wheel of fortune lady picks up the trays of money and unstacks them.

WHEEL OF FORTUNE LADY (*looks at assistant manager*): Thirty-five thousand on number twelve.

Roy comes up from background.

ROY: Do me a favor, willya, honey, put a thousand on number twelve. (*Puts a money clip with one thousand dollars on the board.*)

ALLEN (*placing his bet*): One hundred dollars on one, one hundred dollars on three, five hundred dollars on twelve, one hundred on twenty-one, . . . the Lord hates a coward. (*Puts black chips down while talking.*)

THÉO (*Allen's girl*): Make a bet for me!

The Texas high roller leans in.

TEXAS HIGH ROLLER: Honey, give me five hundred dollars on twelve.

ANDY Give me twenty dollars on twelve.

BURT (*who has meanwhile been trying to get Andy's attention*): Doc! Doc! . . . Hey Doc, loan me fifty.

ANDY: Fifty on twelve!

WHEEL OF FORTUNE LADY: Thank you, bets are closed.

THÉO: One dollar on number twelve.

WHEEL OF FORTUNE LADY: Alright. Thank you, bets are closed.

Wheel of fortune lady turns and spins the wheel.

WHEEL OF FORTUNE LADY: Aaaaannnnnddddddd . . . Round and round she goes. Where she stops, nobody knows. Good luck to you all.

Everyone in the casino is gathered around the wheel of fortune.

The wheel is spinning.

ANDY: Come on now baby, come home to papa.

ROY: Yes, yes, yes.

The wheel is slowing down.

BURT: Oh please.

TEXAS HIGH ROLLER: Twelve!

ALLEN: One time, twelve, one time.

ROY: That's right.

   Insert. Wheel.

The wheel is about to stop.

WHEEL OF FORTUNE LADY: And the number is . . .

It stops briefly on twelve. Then it jumps over and settles into seventy-four.

WHEEL OF FORTUNE LADY: Seventy-four. The number is seventy-four. No winners on seventy-four.

The crowd sighs, starts to disperse.

The Texas high roller is left at the counter with Gino. He leans in.

TEXAS HIGH ROLLER: Helluva bet, son . . .

He walks away.

The wheel of fortune lady leans over.

WHEEL OF FORTUNE LADY: I'm sorry you lost all that money, sir.

GINO (*takes five-dollar chip out of pocket, hands it to her, shrugs*): Things change . . .

Gino turns and pauses a moment. Then the wheel of fortune lady continues to clear the table. Gino walks across the room toward Jerry and the assistant manager.

ROY (*to Jackie Shore*): What did he say?

JACKIE SHORE: "Things change."

Gino is intercepted by the cocktail waitress who took his order. He shoots the Scotch, tips her. He walks over to Jerry. They look at each other. Gino smiles.

Interior: Night Club—Night

   Camera on two maître d' types.

MAÎTRE D' 1: Give these people something special down front.

MAÎTRE D' 2: Excellent. Right this way.

Camera follows maître d' and the couple, revealing Jackie Shore on stage.

JACKIE SHORE (*delivering his lead-in joke*): I'll tell you what's crazy, folks, the longer I'm married the more I'm losing my single instincts. I was at this Hollywood party, big show-business party, and a beautiful blond starlet comes up to me. She says my husband's away for the weekend, how about a lift home. I said if you knew he was out of town you should've made travel arrangements . . .

The crowd laughs.

Camera finds Gino and Jerry at a table. A cocktail waitress gives them drinks.

JERRY: Thanks.

They continue to listen. Then Gino takes a sip of his drink.

JERRY: How's your drink?

GINO: Good. Good.

JERRY: Well, you handled yourself very graciously back there.

GINO: When in Rome, we do what the Romans do.

JACKIE SHORE (*monologue*): My theory is—criminals wanta get caught. The reporter says eighteen of twenty suspects arrested are known to have organized crime ties. If they don't wanta get caught, don't wear the ties. You know what I'm saying?

Hey, last night I come home with lipstick on my collar and my wife calls it cheating. I call it extramarital fidelity. Call a spade a spade. Be honest. Honesty may not be the best policy, but it's the only one that's got its own proverb. (*There is a muck-up with the lighting guy and Jackie loses his spot. He steps back into the light and tries to regain his audience's attention.*)

I saw a guy today down at the tables, shot thirty-five grand, one roll, craps out. He shrugs, says "Things change." One thing that doesn't change is friendship. Wanta introduce you to a friend of mine. We have a celebrity in the audience, friend of ours from Chicago, Mr. Johnson. Mr. Johnson, stand up, will you? Folks, can you let him know, please? Mr. Johnson, welcome to Tahoe.

Angle. Gino and Jerry. At this point the spot roams the audience, hits Gino. He stands up, nervously, looks to Jerry. Jerry slumps a bit in his seat. Gino waves to the crowd.

JACKIE SHORE (*continuing his monologue*): Take it from me, folks, there's nothing better than friendship, cause if there *was*, somebody would've invented it already . . .

Interior: Backstage—Night

Jackie Shore's set is being struck; the set for the "Egyptian Number" is being set up.

The stage manager is being followed by Jackie Shore.

JACKIE SHORE: Have you got a minute? Hey, have you got a minute? Am I getting this again? Why am I getting this again?

STAGE MANAGER: Mr. Shore . . .

JACKIE SHORE: I walked out of my light. What is your guy doing up there?

STAGE MANAGER: I . . . can't talk to you now.

JACKIE SHORE: What is your lighting guy, your wife's cousin?

STAGE MANAGER: Jackie . . .

JACKIE SHORE: Oh, now it's "Jackie." What, did I do something to you in a previous *life*? What is this? What did I ever *do* to you . . . ?

STAGE MANAGER: Jackie . . .

Gino comes in, following Jerry, who is looking for Jackie Shore.

JERRY: Hey!

JACKIE SHORE: What a nice surprise. Hope you guys enjoyed the show. Mr., Mr. Johnson, . . . good of you to play along, 'preciate it, very sportive of you. You look great up there . . .

JERRY: I thought I told you I didn't want any *publicity*, we don't want any "notice" . . .

JACKIE SHORE: Any notice . . . I, I, hey look, if I "jumped wrong," hey, if you don't want any "notice" . . .

The end of the showgirl procession that has been coming down the staircase passes. Gino and Jerry are looking at them as they go on stage. The last two in line are Cherry and Grace dressed in very abbreviated Egyptian costumes. Gino and Jerry ogle them.

Maybe a *little* notice, eh . . . ? (*He follows them.*) Cherry, Grace, come over here, willya, this is Mr. Johnson from Chicago and this is . . .

The stage manager interrupts and sends the girls on stage. They turn and look back. Jerry and Gino look at the girls.

Photo by Stephen Vaughan

Photo by Stephen Vaughan

Photo by Stephen Vaughan
Photo by Stephen Vaughan

Photo by Stephen Vaughan

Photo by Stephen Vaughan

Photo by Stephen Vaughan

Photo by Stephen Vaughan

Photo by Stephen Vaughan

Photo by Deana Newcomb

Photo by Deana Newcomb

Photo by Deana Newcomb

Photo by Deana Newcomb

Interior: Roman Bath Hot Tub—Night

Angle. The rim of the tub. Grace's head comes over. Camera tracks with her, her head nestles on a leg covered by a towel. Gino's hand comes down and caresses her hair. She looks up.

Angle. The two of them, Gino on the edge of the tub, draped in a toga of towels. We hear a door open. Gino turns.

Angle. Jerry, a towel around his middle, and Cherry, a bath-robe around her shoulders, coming out of the star suite. Jerry holds a bottle of champagne. They walk toward Gino. Jerry holds out the champagne to him, as Cherry moves out of the frame.

Angle. Gino. His eyes wander to Cherry, whose shoulder we just see passing through the frame. His eyes rest on her for a moment, then turn back to Jerry.

Angle. Jerry, sitting down next to Gino, receives Gino's looks of admiration, and then nods as if to say—"Yours ain't bad either." Gino acknowledges this. They both look toward the girls.

Beat.

JERRY (*softly*): I always wondered where I was meant to be.

GINO (*softly*): Is good to *work*, Jerry, is also good to *play*.

Angle. The four, assembled, Gino and Jerry on the rim of the tub, Cherry and Grace in the water.

GINO: The Ant and the Grasshopper. Once upon a time, eh, there's an *ant*, a *grasshopper*. All summer long the ant, he work hard, the grasshopper he (*gestures*), he play the violin. He dance.

GINO (*voice-over*): Winter come . . .

Cherry and Grace both look attentively at the storyteller.

   Angle. The four.

GINO: The ant grow fat, the grasshopper is a-*cold* . . .

   Angle. The three and Gino.

Beat.

GINO: The grasshopper, he eat-a the ant.

All listeners pause, then nod, appreciatively.

The two girls swim to the next corner of the tub. As they turn Gino starts to sing a love song in Italian. Jerry sings along in English.

He gives Gino the bottle of champagne.

JERRY: Bravo, Gino. *Canto bello.* [You sing beautifully.]

GINO: *Grazie, grazie.*

Meanwhile, the girls whisper.

CHERRY: Uh, you guys like the water?

Gino and Jerry turn to look at her.

JERRY: Whattya have in mind?

   Angle. The four.

CHERRY: Uh, we have a little cabin, up on Fallen Leaf, and, uh, we're going to go fishing for a few days. Would you, we wanted to know if you want to come there and go fishing with us. Really fishing.

GRACE: For fish.

CHERRY: Tomorrow. When we get off.

Beat.

JERRY: We have to be back in Chicago.

CHERRY: Well, you know, *any* time . . .

GRACE: Any time you come in . . .

CHERRY: . . . that you wanted to come up, anytime that you're in Tahoe . . .

GRACE: Next time you're back here.

   Angle. Jerry and Gino.

Beat.

JERRY: We might not be back here for a while.

GINO: We gonna be gone for a while . . .

GRACE: Anytime. Six months, a *year* . . .

Gino and Jerry take a look.

JERRY: Well, it actually might take longer than that.

GINO: We gonna be gone for quite a while, dear girls.

Interior: Hotel Suite

A rumpled bed. Beat. We pan across, something is stirring under the covers. It is Jerry. He sits up.

Floor level: Pile of rumpled clothes. Legs come over the side of the bed. Jerry picks up his clothes. We pan up with him as he stands up, carrying his clothes.

In the living room: We pan with Jerry as he comes out of his room, looks around, looks out the window, takes a deep breath. He does a kneebend, walks over to the coffee table, dropping his clothes.

   Insert. He picks up a note from the girls, which reads "If you change your mind about fishing, give us a call. Cherry & Grace. KL 5-2560."

Jerry carries the piece of paper. We pan with him over to the telephone. He puts the note on the arm of the sofa. He picks up the telephone.

JERRY: Good morning. (*Beat.*) Would you be so kind as to send us up some coffee . . . ? (*Beat.*) Lovely. Thank you very much.

Jerry looks in the mirror, adjusts his hair. He walks toward Gino's room singing in Sicilian.

Aiu un *cappiduzzu*—Hey Gino, wake up and smell the coffee . . .
Veramenti sapuri tu
Quannu me l'aiu mettari
Quannu me fazzu zitu . . .

He turns back and looks at the room.

This is the kind of *day* . . . Listen and learn something . . .

He turns into Gino's room.

   Inside Gino's room: Jerry turns into the doorway.

This is the kind of day . . .

He stops, looks around.

   Jerry's point of view. Empty room.

   Close-up on Jerry. Alarmed.

Gino . . . ?

Jerry runs back through the living room picking up his clothes.

Interior: Hall

Jerry comes out the door dressing. He looks up.

   *Jerry's point of view. The chambermaid at the next door with
   her cart.*

CHAMBERMAID: Good morning, sir.

JERRY: Good morning.

CHAMBERMAID: I hope you and Mr. Johnson slept well.

JERRY: Yeah, just great.

CHAMBERMAID: Anything special you need in your room, sir?

JERRY: No, can't think of a thing.

She goes back into room. Jerry continues dressing himself in the hall.

Gino and Randy in the shoe room.

GINO: You rub too hard, then you . . .

RANDY: You take off the polish.

GINO: So the trick is . . . ?

RANDY: Not too hard and not too soft.

GINO: And you can't make a good shine unless . . .

RANDY: . . . the shoes are clean.

Jerry is a little bit more dressed. He starts down the hall looking for Gino. He stops at the gates.

He suddenly hears voices and slows down.

   Off-screen dialogue:

RANDY: The shine comes from underneath.

GINO: That's right.

RANDY: I wonder why I never noticed that before.

GINO: Hey, if everyone knew everything, there wouldn't be no school, eh?

RANDY: Yes?

GINO: Shine-a shoes like anything else . . .

Jerry continues down the hall. He sees Gino and Randy in the shoe room.

RANDY: It seems so simple now.

GINO: Yes and no . . .

RANDY: I'm really sorry, Mr. Johnson.

GINO: No be sorry. Live and learn. (*He hands Randy his apron.*)

JERRY: Where have you been?!?

GINO: I leave my shoes outside, they come back dull.

Jerry goes to Gino, grabs him by the arm, and takes him back down the hall.

JERRY: You don't go anywhere, *anywhere*, do you hear me . . . ? *Anywhere* without me. We're goin' back today.

GINO: I just go down the hall.

JERRY: We're goin' back to Chicago today.

GINO: *Why . . . ?*

JERRY: You can't obey orders!

Jerry grabs him and pulls him inside, closing the door.

Interior: Star Suite—Day, the Main Doors

The doors open; Jerry, followed by Gino, enters.

JERRY: Get your stuff. We're out of here—we're goin' back to Chicago.

GINO: I can't go back to Chicago.

JERRY: Who the hell do you think you are? I stepped out of channels, I put myself out for you, what did you do for me? What'd I say? One thing: obey orders, stick by my side . . . one thing, n'you couldn't do it. You see? I was *your* friend, but you weren't *my* friend. The hell with you. Go back to Sicily, go back to prison, I don't care, but we're goin' to Chicago.

GINO: I can't go back to Chicago.

JERRY: Don't you *tell* me what you can and cannot do. You're *nothing*, pal. You belong to the Organization, you belong to *me*. Pack your stuff.

GINO: I can't go back to Chicago.

JERRY: Is that so? Why *can't* you go back to Chicago?

GINO: I don't have my shoes.

A knock on the door. Randy enters, hands Gino his shoes.

GINO: Thank you.

Randy closes the door. Beat. Gino and Jerry look at each other, Jerry exits, followed by Gino.

Interior: Hotel Room

JERRY: Catch me ever doing a favor for *anyone*.

GINO: You mad at me.

JERRY: *Mad* at you? Yeah, if I came back without you, they'd *kill* me. You think that's a joke?

GINO: I got no answer. I gave my word.

Jerry buzzes for the butler.

JERRY (*into intercom*): Can we get some coffee in here . . . ?

GINO: . . . I'm on the corner, four P.M., he's drive a big black car, a Lincoln . . . He comes on the *street* . . .

JERRY: Okayokayokay.

GINO: He's come on da street, I shoot that sonof . . .

JERRY: Okay. Okay. Fine. Yeah. What do you want to do today? Let's get out of here. Let's do something.

GINO: We see those nice girls . . .

JERRY: Yeah. Don't take that "we go fishing" line too seriously. Okay? Everything's for sale in this town, everybody loves ya when ya got the dough.

GINO: No, they liked us.

JERRY: Yeah. They liked us real good—everybody likes you when you're somebody else. (*He takes out his wallet, checks his bankroll, replaces wallet in jacket.*) We have one day left. We have one day's worth of a good time. Then we go home.

There is a knock at the doorway.

Come in! (*He stands up.*) Okay? I'll get dressed, let's get outa here, and you stick by my side. (*He starts for the other room, and turns to see who is in the doorway.*)

Angle. In the door, Billy Drake, the driver from the airport.

BILLY DRAKE: Jerry, there are two *friends* of ours . . .

He stands aside. Two burly, well-dressed organization men enter the room.

Kenny and, uh . . .

HARRY HARDWARE (*a Tahoe thug*): Thank you, Billy.

Billy Drake bows himself out. The two step into the room, and respectfully approach Gino, who puts down his list, looks up at the two men.

KENNY (*a bodyguard*): Mr. Johnson . . . ?

Gino nods.

Joseph Vincent sends you greetings and welcome to Lake Tahoe. He extends to you this invitation: to be his guest at his Estate at Lake Tahoe for luncheon today, if this is convenient with your plans.

JERRY: Well, you know we have a lot of . . .

Kenny gives Jerry a withering look.

KENNY (*to Gino*): If this would be convenient. One P.M. We'll pick you up downstairs. We'll be waiting for you in the lobby.

The two organization men respectfully leave the room. Beat.

JERRY (*slowly*): We're in some very. deep. shit.

Interior: Large Limo—Backseat—Day

Jerry and Gino alone in the backseat. Jerry is whispering frantically to Gino.

JERRY: Okay, now: look: look: look: Whatever he *asks* you, say . . .

Gino nods—"Yes, guide me."

Uh . . . No. No. Whatever he . . . Ah. You're on Vacation! You . . . you're on, you don't want to *talk* no business, you don't want to *hear* no, so, so when we *get* there, it's like . . . If he asks you "Who You Are . . ."

Gino, very nervous.

. . . just, just . . .

Jerry stops Gino's fidgeting.

Just . . . Let *me* handle it. Whatever it *is*, I'll, I'll . . .

Interior: Don Vincent's Kitchen—Day

Camera on pot lid, drops to reveal close-up of Anna tasting soup. She turns to a cook next to her.

ANNA: *Mete un po di sale.* [Put in a little salt.]

She goes to the white stove and starts checking the vegetables. Kenny, who is seated with a list, gets up and walks to table where Harry Hardware and Billy Drake are seated, having just finished lunch.

KENNY (*hands him list*): Approved list, the vehicles . . .

HARRY HARDWARE: I'm on top of it.

Kenny goes to the stove and tastes something.

You got a load of vegetables coming in at *four o'clock.*

KENNY: From where?

HARRY HARDWARE: Reno.

KENNY: Stop 'em at the gate and call me . . .

Anna has come over to the table with two cups of coffee. Two guys come in with a crate of wine. One guy off screen says "eh?"

Anna?

ANNA: *Vor due ancore, portalo dentro la.* [You two again, bring it in there.]

KENNY: Put it in the pantry.

Kenny goes to the door, buttons his coat, leaves as the Don's houseman comes in with a tray of dirty dishes. The two guys with the crate of wine cross the room to the pantry and put it down. Anna gets Kenny's dirty plate, crosses to the counter of dirty dishes and intercepts the Don's houseman.

ANNA (*to the Don's houseman*): *Senti, prendi, una bottegli di grappa. Presto, via.* [Listen, bring in a bottle of grappa. Hurry up.]

He moves out of the room, she follows, meeting an Italian woman in the doorway.

ITALIAN WOMAN: *Gli carciofi?* [What do I do with the artichokes?]

ANNA: *Casa peusi.* [Steam them, naturally.]

Anna crosses back across the room and gives the cook instructions.

Maria, pulire la tabola, sulsi to. [Maria, clean the table immediately.]

The two men who had the crate walk back across the room and out.

Grazie. Ciao. [Thanks. So long.]

HARRY HARDWARE (*yells out to the men who just left*) I want to talk to you about the Chevy!

Anna yells something to someone off screen.

ANNA: *Santuzza, il pane t'aspetta.* [The bread is waiting.]

She crosses to get a tray and some glasses for the grappa.

Billy Drake and Harry Hardware are smoking cigarettes and start a conversation.

HARRY HARDWARE: A dealer at the Stateline . . .

BILLY DRAKE: This is the swing-shift broad . . . ?

HARRY HARDWARE: Used to go out with whatsisname . . . the *big* guy . . .

BILLY DRAKE: Who is this . . . ?

HARRY HARDWARE: The *big* guy . . .

BILLY DRAKE: Oh, right, right . . .

HARRY HARDWARE: Okay, now, so she's torn between two guys . . .

BILLY DRAKE: She's hiding the sausage with both of them . . .

HARRY HARDWARE: She's the one.

BILLY DRAKE: And you're saying she's the one that stabbed him?

HARRY HARDWARE: The same one. Knocked the other guy's teeth out.

During this dialogue Anna has put a tray on the table. The Don's houseman brings her a bottle of grappa. She pours two glasses.

Camera has panned off them during the dialogue onto close-up of tray, then a close-up of her as she picks up tray. She looks off screen at something. She leaves room.

   Anna's point of view. Jerry is at the window looking out.

   Jerry's point of view. He sees the Don and Gino seated through another window. Anna comes in with tray.

Jerry is concerned.

HARRY HARDWARE (*off screen*): Hey, Jerry, what's a good price for a '56 Chevy?

JERRY (*turns to him*): Yeah. (*Turns back to window.*)

Interior: Don Vincent's Study.

Lunch remnants on the table. Anna comes in with a tray of grappa and puts it on the coffee table.

ANNA: *Volete fumara adesso?* [Do you want a smoke now?]

Don gestures—"no." Anna walks away. The Don and Gino move from the table to the fireplace area. They sit. After Anna gets out of earshot, Don speaks.

DON VINCENT: It's good to know one's family. (*Beat.*) A good man prides himself on knowing those who are connected to him. Would you agree?

GINO: I have a very large family.

DON VINCENT: . . . and no matter how large our families are, still we remember all their names.

Gino nods sagely.

GINO: From the smallest to . . . (*He gestures with his hand.*)

The Don nods his agreement.

DON VINCENT: So. Tell me some names.

Beat.

GINO: . . . names of my family?

The Don nods.

Uh, Bruno Gatto and *little* Bruno Gatto.

Beat. Kenny appears from behind a column, stands menacingly in the back of the room.

DON VINCENT (*smiles, sadly*): I don't know them.

Beat.

Do you see what I mean? What brings you here?

GINO (*apologetically*): I am not here to talk business.

DON VINCENT (*shrugs*): We'll talk business *later.* But I must know. What brings you to this occasion?

The Don finally signals to Kenny, who comes forward a bit. The Don gets up. Kenny takes a dagger out of a sheath behind his back, glides up on Gino.

Gino also gets up, takes the Sicilian coin out of his pocket, fiddles nervously with it.

The Don looks at Gino and the coin.

What a lovely old coin. (*Beat. To Gino, as if throwing him a cue:*) Is There Anything That You Can *Tell* Me About It?

GINO (*beat; nervously*): A Big Man Knows the Value of a Small Coin.

The Don moves to Gino.

DON VINCENT: It's always good to make a new friend . . .

He shakes Gino's hands and pulls back his T-shirt sleeve revealing a tattoo on his right forearm. The tattoo is the same face and inscription as are on the Sicilian coin that we just saw. Gino reacts.

He then leads Gino over to the front of the fireplace.

He motions Kenny, who walks over, hands them grappa glasses, and leaves.

GINO (*gives a toast in Sicilian*): . . . *L'amicu mui du me cori.* [Friend from my heart.]

Beat. The Don is very moved.

DON VINCENT (*feelingly*): I haven't heard that in thirty-five years.

They toast and drink. The Don smashes his glass into the fireplace followed by Gino. They embrace.

> *Angle—Interior. Kitchen. Jerry, still watching them out of the kitchen window. He is completely bewildered by what he sees.*

Exterior: Don Vincent's Estate

> *Insert. A drawing of a sailboat in the sand.*

Gino and the Don are sitting on the beach, drinking, looking out.

GINO: *E'gran pazzia lu cuntrastari* . . . [It is crazy to compare oneself . . .]

DON VINCENT: *cu cu' nun po vinciri ne' appattari* . . . [with he whom you cannot beat or equal . . .]

Gino nods. He picks up a small stone.

GINO: I'll bet you one million dollars I can hit that rock.

DON VINCENT: If I win, what? If I lose, what? (*Beat.*) Alexander the Great conquered the world, and then cried because there were no new worlds to conquer.

Gino (*shrugs*): He was-a young.

They look out.

> *Point of view: A sailboat tied to the dock. Their shoes and jackets in the sand.*

You have beautiful shoes.

DON VINCENT: Even the best shoes wear out. Things change.

GINO: With care they last a long time, you watch closely . . . you watch for the crack.

DON VINCENT: And then . . . ?

GINO: And then you watch more closely.

Beat. The Don considers, nods.

Show me you boat.

Gino gets up and helps the Don to his feet. They pick up their shoes. Jerry, seated on the land, looks on.

> *Jerry's point of view: The Don and Gino on the dock walking toward the boat.*

> *Frontal shot of Gino and the Don walking toward the boat. The Don sighs, takes out his cigarette case.*

You tired, Don Giuseppe . . .

DON VINCENT: Well, you know, you know how it becomes . . . the pressure.

Gino nods.

GINO: I tell you something. You alright. (*Beat.*) You trust an old man . . .

Longer shot. The two walking toward the boat. An attendant in the fishing shack on the pier motions the Don back toward the end of the dock. He and Gino turn.

Point of view: Kenny at the foot of the dock beckoning the Don, holding a telephone. He gestures—"This is a very important call. I don't know if I should be interrupting you or not . . ."

The Don nods—"I'll be right there." The Don looks at Gino. Gino shrugs, the sailboat in the background.

The Don offers Gino a cigarette. Gino takes one. The Don starts to take a cigarette from the case for himself. Gino's hand stops him. Beat. Gino takes his own cigarette, breaks it in half, hands half to the Don, who takes it and smiles. The Don takes his gold lighter and lights both cigarettes. (The lighting of the cigarette covered in over-the-shoulders with the sailboat behind Gino, Kenny behind the Don.)

DON VINCENT: You'll stay tonight, stay with me, tonight. After dinner we'll talk. Will you stay?

New angle. Gino and the Don against the fishing shack.

GINO: You offer me your home. What can I give to you . . . ?

The Don gestures—"You've given it." They start toward land. Gino stops him, reaches in his pocket.

Insert. Gino's hand, taking out the old Sicilian coin.

Single Gino: offering the coin to the Don.

Da un'amico a un'altro. [From one friend to another.]

Single the Don: accepting. Nods. Reaches in his pocket.

DON VINCENT: This is not an old coin. It is a new coin.

Insert: The Don takes a fly out of a fly-fishing box, puts in the quarter, writes his number inside the top of the box, turns.

But it, too, is a symbol. And should you ever need my friendship, you put this coin into a telephone. You call this number. Whatever you wish, if it is within the power of your friend, that wish shall be granted.

Gino takes the coin. They walk away.

Exterior: Don Vincent's Estate

Gino, and the Don walk toward the house, their arms around each other. Kenny follows at a respectful distance.

   Side angle.

DON VINCENT: Hey, Gino, you got grass stains on your best pants! Your momma's going to kill you.

They both laugh.

(*To Kenny:*) Have Mr. Johnson's things cleaned and sent to his room . . . (*To Gino:*) We'll talk tonight, after dinner. (*To Kenny:*) Mr. Johnson will be staying with us tonight.

Jerry comes running up.

JERRY: Uh, as much as we'd like to *accept* the *hospitality* . . .

The Don and Gino turn around, the Don aghast at this breach of etiquette. His look brings Jerry up short. The Don gestures to Gino, as if to say—"Isn't this just what we were talking about . . ." Gino shrugs to indicate—"You're absolutely right, what are you going to do?"

GINO: I put him on probation.

The Don nods in agreement, as if to say—"Yes, but we both know it won't help."

They walk on.

The Don and Gino continue to walk toward the house.

Camera stays on Jerry.

DON VINCENT: We're having some *people* tonight . . . perhaps you know some of them. We'll have a nice dinner . . . we'll talk about "shoes." *Tomorrow,* we go fishing. *(To Gino:)* Anything else you need, you talk to my people. *(To Kenny:)* Whatever Mr. Johnson requires, see that he *has* it—otherwise see that he is not disturbed.

The Don and Gino continue toward the house. Jerry, looking on, amazed.

The Don and Gino walk toward the house, stepping up onto the path.

DON VINCENT: Gino, you like "fighting" fish? I'm going to show you some northern pike tomorrow. First we're gonna *catch* 'em, then we're gonna *cook* 'em!

Halfway up the path Gino takes a look back at Jerry. They continue up, the Don taking a phone from the houseman.

KENNY: Come on, we're goin' over the hotel.

Interior: Chevy Station Wagon—Day

Kenny driving. Jerry sitting next to him. Jerry silent. Beat.

KENNY: So. (*Pause.*) How, uh, how heavy *is* your guy . . . ? I mean, I never seen the Don pal *up* that close with someone like that before . . . (*He casts a glance at Jerry:*) Unless it's something I shouldn't *know* . . .

Jerry gives him a withering glance. Beat.

What are they? Friends from the *Old* country? (*He gestures—"I know I've been off-base." Jerry is seething, Kenny puts his attention back on his driving.*)

Exterior: Entrance Galaxy Hotel—Day

The Chevy station wagon comes up to the curb. Car park attendant takes the car. Kenny and Jerry get out, start into the hotel.

   Angle. Kenny and Jerry entering the lobby.

BELLHOP: So how are you and Mr. Johnson today, sir?

KENNY (*to Jerry*): You know, we don't got to do this, c'mon, we'll get a cup of coffee . . .

They walk over to the check-in desk. Kenny hits the bell.

Somebody check out Mr. Johnson.

BELLHOP (*repeats*): Check out Mr. Johnson . . . (*Checks files.*)

From the hall, the manager appears.

MANAGER: Front! Front! Check out Mr. Johnson.

Jerry, livid, turns.

The manager goes back toward the door to the hall. Jerry follows.

Angle. In the hall Jerry pushes the manager against the wall.

JERRY: What are you doing? What the *hell* are you doing . . . ?

MANAGER: I . . .

JERRY: I told you no, we want to keep a low profile . . . you, you, *you* . . . what are you crawling all over us, the whole time, *you* don't know who . . . "Mr. *Johnson*" . . . Whaddaya . . . you don't know who Mr. Johnson is . . .

MANAGER: I . . .

JERRY: You what? You what? Do you know what we're doing here?

MANAGER: I . . .

JERRY: What . . . ?

MANAGER: I thought you were here for the meeting.

JERRY: *What* meeting?

Suddenly Jerry hears a bellhop.

BELLHOP: Check in Mr. Green! Check in Mr. Green! From Chicago!

Jerry turns. He starts walking toward the door.

Angle. The Chicago entourage enters. Scarface (the bodyguard), Mr. Green, Miss Bates, Silver, and another bodyguard.

MR. GREEN: What time are we due at Joe Vincent's house?

SILVER: Eight o'clock. You just have time to change.

MR. GREEN (*to Miss Bates*): You look lovely. (*He kisses her. To Silver:*) Check us in. I'll be at the tables.

SILVER (*to clerk*): Mr. Green's party is here. Do you have the two cars?

CLERK: Yes sir.

SILVER: Is the champagne in his room?

CLERK: Yes sir.

SILVER: Line of credit in the casino?

CLERK: Yes sir.

SILVER: I don't want him showing I.D. around here.

CLERK: Yes sir.

Jerry continuing to watch all this, shutting the door and looking through the window in the door.

He turns back.

JERRY: Oh heck.

Interior: Don Vincent's Dining Room

Anna surveys the room. She moves across it as a man is putting candles in the living room. Another man is putting a vase of

*flowers on a ledge near the stairs. The Don's houseman is passing by
with a lighter and silver box.*

ANNA: *L'acendino carico?* [Is the lighter filled?]

The Don's houseman nods "yes."

*She continues on to the table. Sarah, a cook, and her daughter Sam
are standing at attention.*

*Anna looks at a glass on the table and nods to it. Sarah imme-
diately nods to Sam, who goes over and starts cleaning the glass
with a towel. Anna continues to the other end of the table. She stops
and checks it out.*

*A lady is standing at attention with a candle. Anna motions to her
to start lighting the candles. Anna turns and walks through the
pantry.*

A guy is cleaning wine glasses.

ANNA: *Apri il vino.* [Open the wine.]

She continues into the kitchen.

Interior: Kitchen

*Anna comes in, passing cooks and bodyguards. Billy Drake is in
there telling a story.*

BILLY DRAKE: . . . Three-ninety-six Chevelle, 1968, sort of a
metallic green, my brother's car—this thing was cherry—brand
new. It had a four-barrel on it—I'm not kidding you—size of a
basketball—you'd punch the throttle on this thing, the hood

would cave in! We used to take it down to this place in Ridgely, West Virginia—the hog trough . . .

Suddenly Kenny pushes his way into the room, quieting Billy Drake. He is followed by Jerry, who stands behind the guards in the hall.

KENNY: Okay!

ANNA: *Tutti fuori della mia cucina.* [Everybody out of my kitchen.]

KENNY: *Una momento.* Sorry I'm late. I've got a couple of things I want to go over with you guys. Number one is the *cut*-off time, which is eight-fifteen, after which *nobody* gets in, if they're at the gate after eight-fifteen they're an Indian. The *second* thing is nobody's anyone unless I introduce you to him, listen closely to me now, it's better you have to apologize to someone, what you said to him, than, huh? You know what I'm talking about, like that time with the guy down at the lake. Ron and Charles, your station is the Front and Back, you keep your eyes on the doors, you let the Perimeter take care of itself. Any of the out-of-town *guys*, some of the guys you know, the rest I'm going to introduce you to. These guys, of course, are our guests, but anybody asks any personal questions about the Don, anything that goes on in this house, what's the correct response . . . ?

BODYGUARDS (*all at once*): We don't know. It's none of your business. I don't know. You're asking the wrong guy.

KENNY: Okay. Chris Centrella. This is you . . .

Interior: Hallway

Jerry goes down the corridor, confused and looking into doors to find Gino.

He finally gets to the correct door, stops, and looks in.

Jerry's point of view. Gino on the bed.

Jerry goes inside and shuts door.

JERRY: Come on . . .

GINO: What?

JERRY: Come on . . . come on . . . we're goin' home . . .

GINO: We don't gotta leave until tomorrow . . .

JERRY: We're cutting short our trip.

He takes the plane tickets out of his jacket pocket, checks them, puts them back in.

We got forty-five minutes to make the plane back to Chicago.

GINO: We still gotta one more day . . .

JERRY: Forget it!

There is a knock at the door. Jerry turns, reacts, crosses to door. The Don's houseman is standing there with Gino's clean clothes. Jerry takes them and shuts door as the Don's houseman leaves. Jerry crosses back to Gino with clothes.

Get dressed! Come on!

Interior: Hallway

Camera follows Jerry and Gino down the hallway and down the staircase. Just as they get close to the bottom, Anna crosses into the living room with a candy tray. They continue downstairs toward the open door. Gino stops, patting his pockets.

JERRY: What? What?

GINO: I forgot my lucky quarter. (*He turns and goes.*)

JERRY: Are you *nuts?* Come on . . .

Gino is running back up the stairs. Anna crosses back through, as Jerry reacts.

Jerry is standing in the middle of the room alone. Suddenly he hears something which makes him turn toward the door.

The Don is outside coming toward the house with Mr. Green, Silver, Miss Bates, bodyguard with gift, and Scarface.

The Don and Mr. Green are heard talking about the weather in Chicago.

DON VINCENT (*just as they reach top step*): Smooth flight?

Jerry runs for door and watches from there.

MR. GREEN: An excellent flight, thank you, no problems . . .

DON VINCENT: They treating you well at the hotel?

MR. GREEN: Just fine. How you feeling?

DON VINCENT: Very well, couldn't be better.

They get to the door and enter.

DON VINCENT: I'm sure you'll find the food here a lot better than at the hotel.

MR. GREEN: That's what I expected.

DON VINCENT: And, Max, the same would be for your place in Chicago.

MR. GREEN: Next time you won't have to bring your lunch.

Scarface has just cleared the door and is crossing the room looking around. Jerry is hiding behind door.

I'd like you to meet my companion, Miss Bates.

DON VINCENT: Miss Bates, you are an adornment to my house.

MR. GREEN: Oh, and I have another one for you.

Jerry goes out of window, avoiding Scarface, who turns and crosses back toward the door.

Mr. Green summons Ned, a bodyguard, with boxed present. He steps forward and opens the box, revealing guns and stuff.

DON VINCENT (*takes gun out*): Extraordinary! 1827?

MR. GREEN: If you say so.

DON VINCENT: Serial numbers filed?

MR. GREEN: You bet.

Scarface has taken his position by the door.

The Don nods to a maid standing in the background. She comes forward to take Miss Bates's coat.

DON VINCENT: Ned, good to see you.

Ned closes box and goes into living room. Maid takes Miss Bates's coat and goes into dining room.

DON VINCENT: Miss Bates, welcome.

She kisses her finger, touches it to Mr. Green's lips, goes into living room.

Gino comes down the stairs.

Silver crosses over to the Don. The Don shakes his hand.

Mr. Silver, welcome.

SILVER: Thank you for inviting me.

Silver goes into the living room.

Scarface gets a nod from Mr. Green and crosses into the living room.

Mr. Green goes for cigarettes in his pocket.

The Don and Mr. Green turn.

DON VINCENT: And there's somebody I'd like you to meet. A friend of ours. (*Looks up.*) Oh, here he is now!

Mr. Green looks up.

Gino takes a Smokey the Bear hat off a hatrack and puts it in front of his face.

GINO: . . . Seven and five-eighths . . . Don Giuseppe, you got a big head.

Mr. Green and the Don laugh.

SILVER (*calling from living room*): Mr. Green, would you come here, I'd like to show you something.

DON VINCENT (*to Mr. Green*): Thank you for the gift.

Mr. Green leaves.

The Don walks forward.

Gino comes downstairs to bottom.

GINO: Don Giuseppe . . .

DON VINCENT: Hope you had a good nap . . .

Willie, the Texas Don, enters.

WILLIE: Joe, good to see you.

DON VINCENT: Willie, good of you to come.

WILLIE: Been too long.

DON VINCENT: Yes it has.

WILLIE: I brought you a little something.

The Texas Don's retainer presents and opens a case containing a bowie knife.

DON VINCENT: Willie, that's magnificent.

WILLIE: Nothing's too good for you, Joe.

DON VINCENT: We'll talk later.

Kenny passes through.

WILLIE: Kenny, good to see you.

Willie goes into living room. Kenny goes out the door. Anna and a woman with a tray of antipasti cross into living room.

GINO: Don Giuseppe . . .

The Don walks to him.

DON VINCENT: I think you'll know who most of these people are . . . a life full of business, eh?

GINO: Don Giuseppe. If I have to leave, all of a sudden—

The Italian Don enters.

ITALIAN DON: Don Giuseppe . . .

DON VINCENT: Giovanni . . .

ITALIAN DON: *Como esta?*

DON VINCENT: *Bene.*

ITALIAN DON: *Ti ho portato una piccola cosa.* [I brought you a little something.]

The bodyguard, Marshall, shows him a mandolin.

DON VINCENT: *Grazie.*

Bodyguards leave with mandolin. Don Vincent and Italian Don embrace.

ITALIAN DON: *Spero che tu viva per mille anni.* [I hope you live for a thousand years.]

The Italian Don goes into living room. Anna crosses back through.

GINO: Don Giuseppe, if I can't stay to go fishing tomorrow—

The Don goes back over to Gino. Howard the New York Don and his party enter.

HOWARD: Joe! Good to see you!

DON VINCENT: Howard, how good of you to come. I know it's a long way.

HOWARD: No trip is too long to pay my respects to you.

DON VINCENT: I really appreciate your coming.

Howard leaves. Meanwhile, the Don's bodyguards file in.

GINO: Don Giuseppe, I have to talk to you.

The Don walks over to him.

MR. GREEN: Joe, come over here, I want to show you something. You're gonna love this.

DON VINCENT (*to Gino*): We'll talk later, soon as they go home.

He goes into the living room. Gino watches him go. The Don joins the group. Gino hears Jerry rapping on the window. He turns back.

   Gino's point of view. Jerry rapping on the window.

Gino turns back to the living room.

   Gino's point of view. Miss Bates lights a cigarette. She looks curiously in his direction. He leaves.

   Miss Bates's point of view. The room without Gino.

Exterior: Don Vincent's—Night

Gino and Jerry come around corner of the house. Gino puts on the Smokey the Bear hat.

They cross the yard. Jerry stops for a moment, takes the hat off Gino, tosses it aside.

JERRY: Will you take off that damned *hat!*

They continue across the yard past limos. Drivers stand around chatting. In the far background Kenny and Scarface come out of the house.

They approach the station wagon. Jerry looks inside. Gino stops and stands in front of the car looking at the house. Jerry gets inside the car. Gino turns and gets into the car. Jerry starts looking for the keys.

JERRY: Okay, okay, okay . . . I'm gonna hot-wire the car. How do you hot-wire a car? You, uh . . . you, uh . . . you cross the, uh . . .

He leans down, pops the hood latch, and gets out of the car. He goes to the front of the car, opens the hood. He takes off his jacket, throws it down, looks under the hood and starts fiddling.

Gino watches him. Then Gino looks through the windshield across to a Cadillac and sees Kenny and Scarface, on a tour of the grounds, approaching them.

He looks on the dashboard and sees the Madonna. He crosses himself.

Then he picks up the Madonna to pray. A car key falls out.

He puts the Madonna back on the dash, moves to the driver's side, starts the car, and smiles at the Madonna.

Jerry closes the hood, runs, and gets back into the driver's side.

The car drives away.

Interior: Station Wagon Driving—Night

Jerry is driving.

JERRY: Okay, we get away clean . . . what's the matter with you? Cheer up . . .

GINO: I'm okay.

JERRY: We're goin' home . . .

GINO: I know where we're going . . .

Suddenly the motor starts to die. Jerry looks at the gas gauge. It reads empty.

What? What?

JERRY: What . . . ? We're out of gas. Guy's the head of the Vegas mob, he can't keep gas in his car. What kind of country is this . . . ?

Jerry looks up and sees something ahead.

  Jerry's point of view. A gas station.

Jerry pulls into the gas station and stops by a pump.

Exterior: Gas Station—Night

Gas station attendant walks to them.

GAS STATION ATTENDANT: Lovely night.

JERRY: Yeah.

GAS STATION ATTENDANT: Fill er up . . . ?

JERRY: How far to the airport?

GAS STATION ATTENDANT: Half a mile. (*He starts for the pump.*)

JERRY (*checking his wallet*): Gimme a dollar . . . maan, I'm runnin' on empty. S'a good thing we're going home . . .

GINO: We was going fishing tomorrow.

JERRY: Who?

GINO: Me and Don Giuseppe.

JERRY: You were going fishing? Don Giuseppe found out who you were, then you were going fishing as the *bait* . . . (*Checks watch.*) S'okay. We're gonna make it. You be thankful you're alive. Anybody talks to you, on the plane, you don't say nothing, you don't even speak English. We get back to Chicago, and this never happened.

The gas station attendant comes over.

GAS STATION ATTENDANT: Five dollars please.

JERRY: I just asked for a dollar.

GAS STATION ATTENDANT: Well, I'm very sorry, sir, I didn't *hear* you.

JERRY: Okay, lookit. S'a misunderstanding, we got a plane to catch. (*Hands the gas station attendant a dollar.*)

GAS STATION ATTENDANT: You owe me four bucks.

JERRY: Yeah, well, we're gonna *send* it to you . . .

GAS STATION ATTENDANT: Love to help you, *can't* . . .

JERRY (*checks watch*): Uh huh . . . uh huh . . . uh huh . . . (*Gets out of car. Confidentially:*) Do you know who this *is* . . . ?

GAS STATION ATTENDANT: Don't know and don't care, but you owe me four dollars.

JERRY: Look, I didn't ask you for the gas, an' I don't got time for this chat, pal, we're sending you the money.

GAS STATION ATTENDANT: No, I think not, mister. Why'nt you stay here till we work this out.

He reaches inside and takes the keys to the car. He walks toward the gas station building. Jerry follows.

JERRY: What the hell do you think you're doing . . . ?

GAS STATION ATTENDANT: I'm calling the cops. Took the gas and you can't pay for it. They call that "theft" . . .

JERRY: Oh, hell, oh, hell, oh, hell, please, please, man, gimme a break, gimme a break, please . . . We've got to catch a . . .

GAS STATION ATTENDANT: . . . treat a workingman like that . . . *you* didn't work for that gas, *I* worked for that gas, I gotta *pay* for it. (*Into phone:*) Lemme talk to th' sheriff. I'll hold.

JERRY: Look, man, look, man, please. *Please.* We have to . . . we have to catch a *plane* . . . please give me the key . . .

Sound of plane taking off. Jerry and Gino look up.

GAS STATION ATTENDANT: I'm holding for the sheriff . . . (*To Jerry:*) Throw your ass in *jail,* tryin' to defraud me.

GINO: What do we do now?

JERRY: We, uh, we, uh, we drive home . . . Uh, uh, *look* . . . look, look, look . . . I have an airline ticket to Chicago. I give you the ticket. I trade you a ticket to Chicago for a full tank of gas.

Beat. The gas station attendant hangs up.

GAS STATION ATTENDANT: You trade me an airline ticket to Chicago for a full tank of gas.

JERRY: You give me a tank of gas and we get out of here.

GAS STATION ATTENDANT: Okay.

Beat. Jerry feels for the tickets.

JERRY: Where's my jacket . . . ?

Beat. Gas station attendant dials the phone.

Gino hears a car drive up. He turns and looks. Gino's point of view of a jeep with several people in it. He walks toward the jeep.

And just when things were goin' so well.

GAS STATION ATTENDANT: Lemme talk to the sheriff . . . (*Into phone:*) I'll hold.

JERRY: . . . and the car's probably stolen, too.

Jerry takes out a pack of cigarettes, opens it, finds it empty, shrugs, to say—"Well, that's quite a shock . . ."

GAS STATION ATTENDANT: You want a cigarette . . . ?

JERRY: No thank you.

GAS STATION ATTENDANT (*into phone*): Hello, Sheriff . . . ? This is Jack down at the Gass tation, got a couple fellows down here . . .

Gino comes back into the frame, lifts up his hand in which he has a fistful of money. He hands several bills to Jerry.

GAS STATION ATTENDANT (*into phone*): Never mind. S'all right.

He hangs up. Jerry gives the gas station attendant a five-dollar bill. The attendant gives him his dollar back with the key.

GINO: We go now.

They get into car and Jerry puts the car into drive and starts to drive out of the gas station. As they come out onto the highway Jerry sees something at the pumps.

Angle—Point of view. The two showgirls, Cherry and Grace dressed for fishing, along with Randy, standing by their jeep. The two girls wave at Gino.

Angle—Interior. Car. Gino nods to the showgirls.

Angle. Jerry and Gino in the car.

The car takes the highway. The showgirls wave.

JERRY: Let's get outta here.

Interior: Station Wagon

Jerry hunched up in front seat covered with his overcoat. Gino hunched up in back seat similarly. They sit for a while not speaking.

GINO: Tell me about it.

JERRY: You *eat*, you *sleep*, you got a *job*, you go and do your job. You don't, you stay in your cell. The time passes, you got the right attitude, the time passes by very quickly.

GINO: . . . It goes by quickly . . .

JERRY: Hey, well, time is *time*, but, *you* know . . . (*Beat.*) And we'll have *people* there for you.

GINO: There'll be people there . . .

JERRY: Yeah, there'll be lots of people there.

GINO: Hey. I can handle it.

JERRY: Don't tell me you can handle it. You never know, until they close that door. And *then* you find out.

GINO (*shrugs*): Well, I'm-a *gone* to find out.

JERRY (*philosophically*): That's right . . .

GINO: An' I get *out*, an' you come see me on my boat.

JERRY: Yeah. I'll come see you on your boat.

GINO: The sun come up we *fish*, the sun go down we *drink* . . . we talk about old times. We talk about Number Twelve! ! !

JERRY: Yeah. Okay.

Beat.

GINO: Is not such a long time . . .

JERRY: No.

Beat.

GINO: So what's the big deal?

Beat.

JERRY: That's right.

Jerry scoots over to the wheel, starts the car, drives away.

Exterior: Desert Road—Night

    Angle—Long shot. The car, alone on a desert road, a billion stars above, the car driving away into the distance.

Interior: Hotel Elevator Bank—Dawn

Jerry and Gino walk down the hallway from camera toward the hotel room.

They get to the door and stop. Jerry puts down the box from the hotel haberdasher's. He takes the key out of his pocket and puts it in the door, unlocking it.

Interior: Chicago Hotel Room

They go into room. Camera follows. It is the original Chicago hotel room. The Kentucky Fried Chicken containers and empty coffee cups unchanged. Beat. They look around. Beat. The gray overcoat hanging on its hanger by the door. They walk around the hotel room for a moment.

Gino stops at the dresser, picks up photo, looks at it, looks at glasses. He puts them down and starts taking off coat.

   Angle. Gino looks up. Gino and Jerry.

JERRY: Well . . .

Beat.

GINO (*shrugs*): Things change . . .

JERRY: What time is it?

GINO: Five, five-fifteen.

JERRY: Well. We got almost five hours. (*Beat.*) Whaddaya want to do . . . ? Naaaaa . . . I don't . . . I . . . Hey, hey, I . . . I wish you didn't have to go.

Gino shrugs—"Me, too."

DON'T GO!

Beat.

GINO: I got to go. (*Beat.*) You know I got to go.

JERRY: No. No. You could . . .

GINO: A deal it's a deal.

JERRY: The hell with the deal. The deal is they're buying three years of your life for pocket change.

GINO: Jerry . . .

JERRY: You're gonna come out of there an old man, buncha money don't mean shit . . .

GINO: *Jerry*— . . . Eh!

JERRY: Eh? Eh? *What* "eh"?

GINO: I got a deal. Three year in prison, I get out, I go back, I buy my boat.

JERRY: You buy your boat. (*Shakes his head sadly.*) You know what your money's goin' to be worth in three years? It won't buy a *toothbrush*, whaddaya, you, whaddaya, you. THREE YEARS OF YOUR *LIFE* . . . ? ? ? You're . . . NO. This is not a *deal* . . . It's a *hustle* . . . they *hustled* you. Three years for three *days* . . .

GINO: I give my word.

JERRY: No, no, you walk. You could *walk* . . . I go in the bathroom. I take—I slip in the *tub*. You walk. Who's going to . . .

GINO: Jerry—

JERRY: Who's going to find you? *No* one. Who's going to . . .

GINO: I . . .

JERRY: Who's going to *look* for you? Go on. Go on! Get *outta* here . . .

He grabs Gino's stuff and throws Gino in the hall.

Get the hell out of here . . . get out of here.

He slams the door. Beat. He lights a cigarette. He goes to dresser. There is a knock at the door. Jerry opens it. Gino comes in.

(*Collapses into a chair, resigned:*) What the hell do you want?

GINO: *Jerry*—we had a good time in Lake Tahoe, eh? We drink the champagne, with the *girls*, Guy on the Stage, says "Mr. Johnson, take a bow."

JERRY: They'd break their word to *you.*

GINO: Maybe yes, maybe no. What they do no matter. I give *my* word. (*Beat.*) I give *my* word. (*Beat.*) I'm going to miss you.

Gino nods.

JERRY: You stupid sonofabitch. (*Shuts door.*)

Beat.

GINO: You gonna miss me, too?

JERRY: I'm not missing no dummy, don't know when to run.

Beat. Gino shrugs.

Do you know what I mean?

GINO: No.

JERRY: Hey, yeah. I'll miss you all my life. Get out of here, you
stupid lame.

Gino has picked up the photo. He heads for the bathroom.

Where are you going?

Gino walks into the bathroom.

GINO: I'm goin-a shave.

Jerry sighs, looks toward the bathroom.

   Angle—Point of view. The bathroom.

*Gino goes in. He sticks the picture of the man who was mistakenly
accused of shooting Aaronberg in the side piece of the mirror. He
takes the tie from around his neck and puts it down. He turns on the
water. He picks up scissors and comb, puts them on the soap tray.*

*He looks at himself in the mirror. He picks up scissors and comb,
puts them to his moustache beginning to fix himself up to more
closely resemble the photo.*

He looks at the photo again. Then he begins clipping.

Interior: Room—Day

   Angle. Jerry is looking out the window at the sun coming up.

   *Angle. Gino, his hair slicked back to look like the murderer. A
   pencil moustache like the murderer.*

*He walks over to Jerry. He looks up at Jerry, smiles, holds out the
photo of the murderer to him—"Look, what a good job I did." Jerry*

*nods. Gino crosses back to the dresser and puts down photo. He goes
to bed, closes haberdasher's box, and puts it under the bed. He takes
his shoeshine box from the floor and puts it on the bed.*

*He puts his jacket on. He goes to the bed beside Jerry and sits. They
look at each other. Jerry watches as he ties his shoes. Jerry takes out a
cigarette, then gives Gino one. He is about to light Gino's when
there is a knock at the door.*

They look up.

Jerry lights his cigarette, stands, and walks to the door. He opens it.

    *Angle—Point of view. It is Frankie, the tough-guy bodyguard
from the first sequence.*

    Angle. Jerry and Frankie from inside the room.

JERRY: What?

FRANKIE: Hey, can I come in?

JERRY: What? Yeah, yeah . . .

Frankie comes into the room.

What are you doing here?

FRANKIE: Come to walk you guys over.

JERRY: We got until ten o'clock.

FRANKIE: They want you there at eight.

Jerry shrugs, acquiesces, Frankie walks around.

Whaddayou guys been *doing* in here three days?

JERRY: Playing gin.

Jerry walks over to Gino.

The guy's here to take us over. (*Beat.*) We're going over early.

Gino nods—"Noblesse Oblige." He looks around the room.

Jerry walks to the door. Gino walks over to Frankie, who has taken the coat off the hanger.

Gino turns as Frankie puts the gray overcoat on him. He picks up his hat. He continues to the door.

He stops in the door a moment. Frankie closes the door.

Exterior: Hotel—Morning

Frankie, Jerry, and Gino come out the hotel door. They stop for a moment on the sidewalk, adjusting coats.

Frankie gestures to Jerry, who nods to Gino. Gino walks across the street followed on each side by Frankie and Jerry.

They continue walking through a nice neighborhood. Jerry and Frankie follow Gino. Gino takes out the letter on Galaxy stationery from the two girls, in which they invited him to go fishing. He opens it and looks at it, then folds it up again.

Frankie, Gino, and Jerry walk down the street and stop at the corner. Jerry starts to turn one way with Gino. Frankie stops them and motions the other way.

FRANKIE: Let's go this way.

Gino walks away folding the paper.

JERRY: Where we goin?

FRANKIE: Hey, I thought we'd take a walk by the Lake. Give him some air in his lungs.

Frankie walks away following Gino. Jerry takes a beat, then follows.

Exterior: Lakefront

Gino walks on the sidewalk with the lake in the background. Jerry and Frankie follow.

FRANKIE: You guys have a good weekend?

JERRY: Yeah.

FRANKIE: Does he know his confession?

JERRY (*sotto*): Yeah. Frankie, what's going on?

FRANKIE: I tol' you, we're taking a walk . . .

At a viaduct. A pedestrian walkway sign reads: This way to the beach.

Angle. They are standing next to the pedestrian walkway, steps leading down, the sun coming up. Gino starts down the stairs. Frankie and Jerry hang back.

JERRY (*to Frankie*): Hey, we got to get to *court.*

FRANKIE (*beat; softly, explaining the obvious*): Jer'—he ain't *going* to court.

Gino proceeds down into the underground walkway.

JERRY: He knows his stuff. He's going to keep his word . . .

Angle—Interior. Walkway. Gino, silhouetted by the sun behind him.

Angle. Frankie and Jerry talking.

He's going to keep his *word* . . .

Frankie shrugs, as if to a child.

FRANKIE (*starts to explain*): Jerry . . .

JERRY: No . . . NO . . .

FRANKIE: Jerry—The thing was: Our guy needed two days to get out of town, this doesn't work. The whole thing was, Set This Guy Up, get his prints on the gun, get a confession: "He's the Guy Who Did It." *Later,* he gets remorse (*points to Gino*), the murder he did. He *kills* himself. We stick the confession in his pocket, life goes on. (*Reassuringly:*) It's cleaner this way.

JERRY: The Don, the Don said: Tell him to be at the twenty-eighth district, ten o'clock *Monday* . . .

FRANKIE: That's right. He said *tell* him to *be* at the twenty-eighth. He didn't say *"Take"* him there.

JERRY (*bluffing tough*): They never told me this was going to be the thing.

Frankie shrugs—"Exactly."

(*Weakly:*) He had a deal.

FRANKIE (*shrugs*): Things change.

JERRY (*pause; starts screaming at Frankie*): You sonofabitch! What the . . . who *are* you, all of you . . . make a *deal* with the man, you . . .

Frankie takes his arm, quiets him, indicates that Gino might overhear them. Jerry lowers his voice.

You set the guy up, *promise* him this . . . *do* the thing . . . The guy does it, he stands *up* . . .

FRANKIE (*quieting him again*): Hey, Jerry . . .

JERRY: Come *on*, come *on* with this, come . . . you're telling me the things you *promised* this guy, *lied* to him, you're going, you're going to turn around and *kill* him?

FRANKIE: I'm not going to kill him. (*Pause.*) You're going to kill him.

Beat.

You're gonna kill him, pal. (*Beat.*) You wanted to square yourself. You got off probation . . . ? What do you think, the thing is "Sit in a hotel room two days order room service," *that's* going to get you back in? *That's* not the job. THIS is the job.

Frankie hands him the scarf-wrapped revolver.

You come up to his head, you shoot him right above the eye. You put the gun in his hand, let it fall.

Beat. Frankie checks his watch.

You got two minutes.

JERRY: You can't make me do this.

FRANKIE: Hey, I'm not making you do *anything*. You turn it down you turn it down. You can't handle it, *I* handle it.

Frankie gives him a little shove, toward Gino.

> *Angle. Gino by the lakeside entrance to the pedestrian walk-way looking at the water. Jerry walks up to him.*

JERRY: Uh, *Gino* . . .

GINO: What?

JERRY: Uh, something happened.

GINO: What?

JERRY: We got a different situation . . . Uh . . . I don't even know how to say it.

Beat. Jerry takes out the scarf-wrapped gun, shows it to Gino. Beat. Gino nods, indicating—"I see."

(*Angrily:*) Didn't I tell you to *run?* I *told* you to run . . . I threw you out the fucken building, you came back. I *told* you to go . . . I *told* you . . . I *told* you . . . Why didn't you *go* . . . ?

GINO: I gave my word.

FRANKIE (*off screen—in the distance*): Hey, Jerry!

JERRY: YOU GAVE YOUR WORD . . . ! ! ! You gave your WORD! ! ! HEY FANTASTIC! ! ! YOU GAVE YOUR . . .

Frankie comes around the corner.

FRANKIE: Hey, Jerry, you gonna . . . !

JERRY: I SAID I'D DO IT, I GAVE MY WORD, EVERYBODY GAVE THEIR GOD DAMN WORD.

Frankie puts his hand on Jerry's shoulder.

Overcome by frustration, Jerry steps in and viciously hits Frankie in the face with the pistol. Frankie goes to his knees.

FRANKIE (*on his knees*): Oh God . . . (*He is crawling on the ground.*) Hey, whaddaya gonna do, whaddaya gonna do now, you gonna shoot *me* . . . ? You gonna shoot *me* . . . ? Shoot *yourself* . . . you're *dead* . . . (*Frankie falls unconscious, on his face.*)

JERRY (*to Gino*): Great, now I'm dead, you're dead, we're all dead. You got the keys to the car . . . ?

GINO: I . . .

JERRY: YOU GOT THE KEYS TO THE CAR? ? ?

Gino starts feeling around in his pockets.

GINO: I only got, all I got . . . (*He takes out the contents of his pockets.*)

Angle—Insert. His hand holding a fly-fishing box he has taken from his pocket.

Angle. Jerry and Gino. Gino holding the box. He opens it.

Angle. The interior of the box. A single quarter. The telephone number Joseph Vincent pencilled on the inside of the lid.

JERRY: WHAT?

Gino turns.

GINO: I'm gonna make a phone call.

JERRY: What phone call?

GINO (*points to the box lid, as he reads and dials the number*): "If Ever You Should'a Need My Friendship . . ."

JERRY: Are you *nuts?* Are you *nuts?*

Jerry gestures—"I surrender." He goes and sits on the stone wall near Frankie, as Gino dials the phone.

GINO (*into phone*): Yes. I like to make a collect call to Mr. Joseph Vincent, from Gino Gatto, in Chicago.

Interior: Courtroom—Day

A bailiff standing in front of the rear doors.

JUDGE (*voice-over*): The defendant having pled guilty to murder in the first degree . . .

The camera pans to the right. Silver is in the last row, watching the proceedings.

. . . and in the absence of Extenuating Circumstances . . .

The camera continues to pan. The Chicago Don, Mr. Green, is sitting next to Silver, looking on.

. . . we have no alternative but to *sentence* the defendant . . .

The camera continues to pan. Jerry is sitting next to Mr. Green and looking on.

   Angle. The judge on the rostrum.

. . . to the maximum allowed by law, a term of imprisonment of twenty years to life.

The judge looks up.

Angle. Gino sitting, looking on.

Angle. The judge again.

Do you have anything to say?

The judge looks to his left. Camera pans to the right to reveal Frankie barbered to look like Gino (and the murderer—i.e., pencil moustache, slicked back hair) dressed in the gray overcoat.

FRANKIE: The car comes on the corner four P.M. I shot the sonofabitch three times in the heart.

Interior: Barbershop—Day

Sicily. The sea. White houses. A fishing boat. A hand reaches through the picture and comes back with a shoeshine rag.

Angle. We see that we are in the shoe repair store. It is the poster of Sicily we have been seeing. Gino has just reached across it for his shoeshine rag. He is on his knees polishing the shoes of a man, who sits on the high shoeshine stand. The man's upper body is obscured by the newspaper he is reading. Beat. Gino finishes the shine. Taps the man on the sole of his shoe. The man lowers the paper and looks down. We see the man is Jerry. Jerry puts down the paper and steps down from the bench. We see that he, too, is wearing a shoeshine apron.

Angle. Gino goes over and picks up another pair of shoes to shine. Jerry gets down, goes over to the same pile and picks up another pair of shoes to shine. They both shine shoes for a moment. Beat. They both look at each other, shrug—"It could be worse." They both turn back to shining shoes.

Fade Out.